A Scho

By the same author

DAILY WE TOUCH HIM
CENTERING PRAYER
Renewing an Ancient Christian Prayer Form
CENTERED LIVING
The Way of Centering Prayer
CALL TO THE CENTER
THOMAS MERTON, MY BROTHER
LIVING IN THE QUESTION
The Questions of Jesus
A RETREAT WITH THOMAS MERTON
AWAKE IN THE SPIRIT
PRAYING BY HAND
LECTIO DIVINA
Renewing the Ancient Practice of Praying the Scriptures
BERNARD OF CLAIRVAUX
A Saint's Life in Word and Image
VATICAN II
THE CISTERCIANS
THOMAS MERTON BROTHER MONK

RHYTHM OF LIFE

Series Editor: Bishop Graham Chadwick

A SCHOOL OF LOVE

The Cistercian Way to Holiness

M. Basil Pennington, o.c.s.o.

CANTERBURY
PRESS

Norwich

Copyright © Cistercian Abbey of Spencer, Inc. 2000

First published in 2000 by The Canterbury Press Norwich
(a publishing imprint of Hymns Ancient & Modern Limited
a registered charity)
St Mary's Works, St Mary's Plain
Norwich, Norfolk NR3 3BH

All rights reserved. No part of this publication which
is copyright may be reproduced, stored in a retrieval
system, or transmitted, in any form or by any means,
electronic, mechanical, photocopying, recording, or
otherwise, without the prior permission of the publisher.

British Library Cataloguing in Publication Data

A catalogue record for this book is available
from the British Library

ISBN 1-85311-343-3

Typeset by Rowland Phototypesetting Ltd,
Bury St Edmunds, Suffolk
Printed in Great Britain by
Cox & Wyman Ltd, Reading, Berkshire

This book is dedicated
to
Dom Clement Kong
the first Chinese Abbot
to
Dom Benedict Chao
who prepared the way
and to
All the Monks of Our Lady of Joy
Lantao, China

Other titles in the *Rhythm of Life* series

THE BOOK OF CREATION
– the practice of Celtic spirituality
Philip Newell

CALLED TO BE ANGELS
– an introduction to Anglo-Saxon spirituality
Douglas Dales

THE CREATIVE SPIRIT
– harmonious living with Hildegard
June Boyce – Tillman

ETERNITY NOW
– an introduction to Orthodox spirituality
Mother Thekla

THE FIRE OF LOVE
– praying with Thérèse of Lisieux
James McCaffrey

LIVING WITH CONTRADICTION
– an introduction to Benedictine spirituality
Esther de Waal

TO LIVE IS TO PRAY
– an introduction to Carmelite spirituality
Elizabeth Ruth Obbard

THE PILGRIM SPIRIT
– an introduction to Reformed spirituality
John Taylor & Helena McKinnon

THE WAY OF ECSTASY
– praying with Teresa of Avila
Peter Tyler

CONTENTS

FOREWORD

My first memory of Basil Pennington is when he visited us in Canterbury and sat at our kitchen table sharing family supper with our four young sons, and talking with contagious excitement about some of his recent monastic journeyings. My most recent memory is of him standing in a large auditorium holding a large audience enthralled as he expounded monastic ideas in a way that touched all of us who were listening. In between I have read and profited from many books of his, all of which reveal his great knowledge and enjoyment of the Cisterican tradition.

These glimpses of his life epitomise so much of what is essentially Cisterican: rooted in the life of an extended family, in all its simplicity and ordinariness, but yet touching hearts and minds with words that make ancient truths new and incisive for succeeding generations. The Cistercians, unlike the Benedictines, have always given us writers, right from the start in twelfth-century Europe with St Bernard of Clairvaux or St Aelred of Rievaulx until our own day when we have Thomas Merton in America and Michael Casey in Australia. Basil Pennington writes from within this tradition, soaked not only in knowledge but love for those whom Thomas Merton so nicely once called 'my Fathers and Friends'.

'Rich, deep, full of wisdom and humour.' What Basil Pennington says of St Bernard could well serve for all those writers he has collected here, as each in turn speaks to us with their own particular voice. But we also hear his own voice too, and that is no less important – a statement about the life and energy of the Cistercian way, as alive and relevant today as it was in those earliest days.

Esther de Waal
March 2000

SERIES INTRODUCTION

'Wisdom is to discern the true rhythm of things:
joy is to move, to dance to that rhythm.'

This series of books on various traditions of Christian spirituality is intended as an introduction for beginners on the journey of faith. It might help us discover a truer rhythm as something of the experience of those who follow any particular tradition resonates with our own.

Too much can be made of the distinctions between the different expressions of Christian spirituality. They all derive from the experience of what God has done and is doing in us and among us. While emphases differ, their validity is their congruence with the good news of Jesus Christ in the scriptures. As the various instruments in an orchestra make their special contribution to the symphony, so we delight in the extra dimension that each tradition brings to the living out of the Christian faith.

The present wide interest in spirituality seems to indicate that, in the midst of all the current uncertainties that we meet in contemporary life, despite its relative comfort and technological advance, there is felt a need to reconnect with our spiritual roots and find a deeper purpose for living.

Each volume offers an introduction to the essential elements of the particular spiritual tradition and practical guidance for shaping our everyday lives according to its teaching and wisdom. It is an exploration into the way that spiritual practice can affect our lifestyle, work, relationships, our view of creation, patterns of prayer and worship, and responsibilities in the wider world.

Many books, of course, have been written in all of these areas and in each tradition classic commentaries are available which can never be surpassed. The aim of this series is to meet the needs of those searching for or beginning to explore the journey inward into their inmost being and outward to relationship with people and the whole creation.

The author of this volume gives us the benefit of his long experience of the Cistercian life and his great knowledge of Cistercian writers. Basil Pennington lets four of the most important figures of this tradition speak mainly for themselves. In chapter six and the appendices, he gives valuable practical help for our sharing in this 'school of love'.

Bishop Graham Chadwick
Salisbury
March 2000

AUTHOR'S PREFACE

There comes up from the depths of every human person a cry and a need for something more in life. Classically Augustine of Hippo, who so profoundly influenced the Cistercian Fathers and the whole Western Christian tradition, expressed it: 'Our hearts are made for you, O Lord, and they will not rest until they rest in you.' The restless heart could well be the symbol of our times, a restlessness that seeks in all sorts of aberrations and infidelity – sexual and otherwise – for what can be found only in faithful pursuit, guided by the divine plan, partially present in nature and graphically set forth in the revelation of Jesus Christ. This inspired and inspiring transcendent realism is what guided the Cistercian Fathers.

It is simply fallacious to assume that the social, cultural and ecclesial distinction between monk/nun and lay person is also a spiritual division. A powerful dimension of Cistercian spirituality is its full acceptance of the human reality – and ultimately the incarnation of God – with all its weaknesses and limitation without ever losing sight of the fact that we are each called in virtue of our creation as the image of God and our recreation in baptism to divinization, full transformation in oneness with Christ, the Son of God.

The richness of the Cistercian school of love is found in the variety of approaches and metaphors used by the four evangelists of Cîteaux – and the many who came after them. While all circled around the father of the school and great master, Bernard of Clairvaux – William of Saint Thierry was his dearest friend, sharing with him most intimately; Guerric of Igny was his disciple, formed at Clairvaux by Bernard; and Aelred was formed through Bernard's secretary, William, the first abbot of Rievaulx – each remained truly himself with his own personal experience of life and the ultimate fulfilment of life. While Bernard could dwell on the Song of Songs and speak of 'visits of the Word', Aelred would seek the Sabbath rest and William, 'unity of spirit'. Guerric, the most down-to-earth and concrete of the four, would avoid using any lofty terminology but constantly point his listeners to the fullness that gave meaning to all the everyday stuff of life.

Beginning with the end – the way we always start a journey – Bernard, especially in his *Sermons on the Song of Songs*, describes in lyric beauty the embrace of divine love in the kiss. Certainly in the course of his writings, which follow the inward and upward path as well as the outward path of his life, he traces out the whole journey, but it is in his sermons on the Song that he shares with us as no other the experience of the fullness of divine union in this life.

Aelred traces out the Christian way in community, in communion with others, in that highest sort of human and divine mutual relationship which we call friendship. But first, as novice master, he wrote a basic manual for beginners, tracing out the whole journey. He particularly gives us insight into the proper integration of the emotional life in our love of both the divine and the human.

It is William of Saint Thierry, who was ever concerned

about the young and their first steps on the journey, who gives us the most extensive systematic guidance for the journey. He, too, begins with the end in view. His first work was on contemplation and then on love. He would comment on the Song of Songs as did his intimate friend, Bernard, but his crowning work, and for most of us his most helpful, is the masterful synthesis that the ages have come to call the *Golden Epistle*.

Finally we look to Guerric not for any systematic treatise but for most practical, down-to-earth guidance in regard to some of the basic details of life such as prayer and work. However, when death suddenly came upon him, he was in the process of putting this practical guidance into the larger context of the way of the Beatitudes.

I don't mean to neglect the Cistercian Mothers, but only a few of them, writing in the second century of Citeaux's growth and expansion, left us a literary heritage. It is a rich heritage and deserves to be set forth as is being done in Sister Lillian Shank's volumes.[1]

While the Cistercian Fathers pointed to and encouraged spiritual experience and transcendence, they did not neglect the need for mature development in other areas of personality. While the psychological terminology found in their treatises, such as William of Saint Thierry's *On the Nature of the Body and Soul* and Aelred's last work, *On the Soul*, may seem primitive, their insight has much to offer us even in the light of modern transpersonal psychology. While they fully recognized our need for healing and wholeness and the potential for spiritual practice to facilitate this (as contemporary medical science is coming to realize more and more) they did not turn the human journey into full Christness into a therapeutic process. What we are called to as men and women baptized into Christ is far beyond this and in God's mysterious design sometimes attained at great human cost.

The brief survey and the texts offered here – their texts themselves are the best introduction to these wonderful persons and their spiritual outlook – are but an appetizer. May they whet your appetite for more. There is a great feast to be found in the extensive literary heritage we have from our Cistercian Fathers and Mothers. The reading list at the end of this slim volume seeks to facilitate finding this nourishment. Cistercian Publications has rendered a tremendous service to the English-speaking world in making these many texts available, including the excerpts to be found in this volume. To all who have laboured in this project I express my thanks.

M. Basil Pennington, o.c.s.o.
St Joseph's Abbey, Spencer
Feast of Saint Gertrude, 1999

I

A SPIRIT IS ENKINDLED

The old monk sat in the wagon surrounded by his bright-eyed, enthusiastic young disciples. Well, not all were quite so young. His alter ego, his right-hand man, Alberic, his prior, had been with him for twenty-eight years and would precede him to the grave. But most were like the bright energetic young Englishman, Stephen: filled with excitement, as they set out on their great venture. Robert found it hard to believe he was on the road again. It had been over fifty years since the spirit of Benedict of Nursia had first enkindled his spirit. And through all those years he did 'truly seek God',[1] beginning each day with the plaintive cry: 'O Lord, open my lips. Let my tongue proclaim your praise.'[2] Zeal for the Work of God, as Benedict called the daily service of praise and prayer, was the hallmark of his life. Moreover he wanted his whole life to be a total 'yes' to the will of God. And to have the freedom for that he wanted, he sought with zeal for a poor and humble life, one free from the ambitions of the world. This was the way of Benedict.

But it was precisely his zeal with its resulting holiness that seemed to frustrate his aspirations. Repeatedly communities called him forth to lead them. But repeatedly he met great disappointment when it became evident that they wanted more the reputation of his holiness than to follow him in the ways of holiness. When the hidden and humble hermits of Collan, including his beloved Alberic, sought his guidance, his hopes were high. And rightly so. He led them to Molesme and established an exemplary monastery where Benedict's *Rule for Monasteries* was held in benediction. But success here also led to the frustration of his aspirations. For the monks' very goodness attracted. Wealth poured in, connections abounded. A humble, hidden life became impossible, especially for the saintly abbot.

Now, seventy though he was, with the blessing of the Papal Legate, he had returned his pastoral staff to the local bishop and was heading with these twenty-one young men to the swampy lands not far from Dijon to begin again. They would build wattle huts to live in and a small stone church in which to praise and live the Rule of Benedict to the full. The excitement that shone in the eyes of his disciples was not absent from his own heart.

That first year was difficult. They knew indeed what it is 'to be poor with the poor Christ'.[3] Their aspirations in that regard were amply fulfilled. But Robert's personal participation in this joy was to be short-lived. The monks of Molesme would not be deprived of their saint. They appealed beyond the Legate to the Pope himself. Robert would have to satisfy his zeal for the work of God in the choirs of Molesme. A clear obedience to the Vicar of Christ himself would chart his course. But his zeal for a humble poverty with its total dependence on God would have to be satisfied with expressing itself in the lives of many others, the young monks of Molesme who would, again and again, set out to face the struggles of new beginnings. His great abbey would send forth ninety-nine such groups until finally the mother-house was laid in ruins by the horrors of the French Revolution.

Robert, himself, would hardly ever express his vision and hopes in writing. Though there is one charter drawn up in his pre-Citeaux days at Molesme that does this in part. Nor would his beloved Alberic be any more productive literally. It was young Stephen, whose intellectual thirst led him from the cloisters of Sherborne to Scotland, Paris and finally to Rome, and whose love for the Benedictine way brought him to Molesme, who would concern himself more with this. Stephen would go so far as to learn Hebrew so that he could personally translate the Bible, to be sure the monks of Citeaux had an authentic text for their lectio – the monastic's daily encounter with the Lord in his inspired word, the foundational element in Benedictine and, indeed, all serious Christian life. In his zeal for the work of God he would send monks abroad and across the Alps to get the most authentic liturgical texts. And he would begin the work of formulating the story of the realization of the vision he shared with Robert and the other founders in an account that has come to be called the *The Little Exordium*.[4] He with his brethren would draft the first constitutions of the emerging Order and get papal approval for this Charter of Charity. But the deep inner spirit that animated all of this, that quest that 'truly seeks God' and expresses itself in a zeal for the 'Work of God', for prayer and praise, that finds its fulfilment in contemplative union – it would be for others to give written expression to this.

We do not know if our blessed Lord Jesus ever wrote a word. But directly and indirectly he inspired his four evangelists to bring his saving message to us in the written form. So to, the Founders of Citeaux had their four evangelists. Stephen himself formed the brilliant and charismatic Bernard of Fontaines, the founding abbot of Clairvaux, in Bernard's year as a novice at Citeaux and during his first year as a monk. And Stephen would continue to guide the young abbot as Bernard emerged as the formative influence in all of Western Christendom. On his visits to Clairvaux the ageing abbot of Citeaux would set his mark on a monk in formation, whose intellectual character was not unlike his own. This monk, Guerric, would become abbot of Igny. But it would be more through Bernard that his spirit would be passed on to this monk and even more so to Bernard's intimate friend, William of Saint Thierry. And it would be through Bernard that their spirit would be carried across the Channel to England to form Stephen's fellow-countryman, Aelred of Rievaulx. We may well imagine that when a mission to Rome brought Aelred to Citeaux, he knelt in prayer at the grave of the venerated founder, grateful that his people were a part of this great spiritual adventure right from the beginning.

In fewer years than it took the monk Robert to reach Citeaux, hundreds of Citeaux's progeny went forth to every part of Europe. The zeal that burned in the hearts of these founders expressed itself with power and eloquence in the words and works of abbots and monks. But, while the intellectual insight and brilliance of an Isaac of Stella might win him a place as the 'St Paul' of Citeaux, it has always remained clear who are the four evangelists: Bernard of Clairvaux, William of Saint Thierry, Guerric of Igny and Aelred of Rievaulx. It is in their writings that we find preeminent expression of the spirit of Citeaux, which inspired the founders to embrace wholeheartedly the evangelical way of the Rule of Benedict with its Christcentredness. And so we now turn to these great spiritual fathers to let each in turn and in his own way speak to us and give us insight into and guidance in the way of the Cistercians which is a school of love.

2

FOR BEGINNERS

William of Saint Thierry

I can hardly justify beginning with William, save that of the four evangelists he is my favourite. Like William I am a bit overawed by Bernard. I do like Guerric's down-to-earthness, but there is not enough of Guerric in the few of his writings that we possess really to get to know him. And Aelred is everybody's friend. William is very much in his writings, the compassionate and concerned father eager to offer help, especially to beginners. So we will begin with him.

In the last days of his life he was occupied with drawing the icon of Cistercian holiness which he had synthesized so well in a treatise-letter he sent shortly before to the Carthusian novices. Indeed it was such a good synthesis of the spiritual journey that it has always been called the *Golden Epistle*. In his *Life of Saint Bernard*, which he undertook at the insistence of many of their mutual friends, William spoke with awe of that encounter thirty years earlier which changed and shaped his life.

At that time William was still young, a monk of Saint Nicaise Abbey in the north of France. He had travelled south on business with his abbot. And now it was time to start for home. They decided on their way to go to see the young abbot of Clairvaux about whom people were beginning to talk. At the time Bernard was in a kind of quarantine, living in a small hut outside the abbey proper, trying to regain his strength. In his excessive zeal he had overdone it and damaged his health for life. William tells us he approached the mean little hut with the same awe with which he approached the altar. Certainly he was moved by what he experienced. He wanted to remain there, a disciple of this holy man. But Bernard was a good judge of character. He saw William had leadership potential and sent him back north to begin the reform of the Benedictines.

Bernard's judgement was confirmed when, shortly after, William was elected abbot of the important Abbey of Saint Thierry on the bluffs above Rheims. William came to his new service filled with the enthusiasm enkindled by what he had seen at Clairvaux. His writings, which began at this time, reflect this as they present the teaching he sought to impart to his monks.

First he set the ideal, the goal, in his relatively short treatise, *On Contemplating God* – surely the ideal and the goal of the Cistercian way. Inspired by Scripture – as these great teachers constantly were – he draws the picture of the spirit leaving the ass, all earthly concerns, behind while he ascends the mountain to worship. With a fine theological mind that betrays his earlier education, William explores the precise meaning of contemplation.

A Vision of Contemplation

William had seen his ideal, the ideal of the monastic life, of all Christian life, incarnate in the saint of Clairvaux. We are called to contemplation, to contemplative union with God.

To begin the journey William calls up a biblical scene
familiar to us all: Abraham's journey to sacrifice Isaac. In
response to the Lord, the Patriarch has set off to the Holy
Mountain, his son at his side, the servant and the donkey
traipsing along behind. When the time comes to ascend to
the Lord, the Patriarch leaves the servant and the donkey
behind. For William this signifies 'worries and anxieties,
concerns and toils, and all the sufferings involved in my
enslaved condition', all of these must 'stay with the ass –
I mean my body – while I and the lad – my intellectual
faculties – hasten up the mountain'.[1]

'Yearnings, strivings, longings, thoughts and affections,
all that is within me, come and let us go up the mountain
or place where the Lord both sees and is seen.'[2]

If we want to come to the experience of God, we have
to be prepared to leave behind the concerns of this world.
William resorts again and again to the words of Psalm 27:
Seek the face of the Lord. But he is realistic. Again reach-
ing for a biblical metaphor he finds Moses, hidden in the
cleft of the rock, seeing only the hind parts of the Lord
and that in a quickly passing experience.

The way up the mountain is the way of love. Here
William reflects Bernard – or does he inspire Bernard? – as
he traces the way: First a due love of ourselves, purifying
and ordering our lives. Then a love of God who is the
source of all the goodness that fills our lives, the God we
find reflected in the creation. From this we rise to a love of
God in God's self, the God so lovable. 'You first loved us
so that we might love you.'[3] And finally we come to love
ourselves and all else only in God and for God, according
as God wills. We come to 'unity of sprit' – *unitas spiritus* –
brought about in us through, in, and with Holy Spirit.

God sent Jesus to us to help us: 'Everything he did and everything he said on earth even the insults, the spitting, the buffeting, the cross and the grace, all that was nothing but yourself speaking in the Son, appealing to us by your love, and stirring up our love for you.'[4]

> This is how you make us love you, love-worthy Lord, or rather, this is how you love yourself in us. We first hoped, because we knew your name, O Lord, we gloried in you as Lord and loved the name of the Lord in you. But now, through the grace of adoption, we invoke you now under the same name as your only Son invokes you by right of nature. . . . We are made one with you just insofar as we are worthy to love you and – as we said just now – become sharers in the fulfilment of your Son's prayer: 'I will that, as you and I are one, so these also may be one in us.'[5]

> We love you and you love yourself in us, we affectively and you effectively, making us one in you, through your own unity, through your Holy Spirit who you have given us.[6]

It doesn't end there. Just as God loves only himself in us, and we have learned to love in ourselves only God, so we are to begin now to love our neighbour 'as' ourselves. For in our neighbour we love God, even as we love him in ourselves.

William attempts to describe the experience of God:

> I draw in the breath of my love, I open my mouth in your direction, I breathe in the Spirit. And sometimes,

Lord, when I, as if with eyes closed, gasp for you like this, you do put something in my mouth, but you do not permit me to know just what it is. A savour I perceive, so sweet, so gracious, and so comforting that, if it were fulfilled in me, I should seek nothing more. But when I receive this thing, neither by bodily sight nor by spiritual sense nor by understanding of the mind do you allow me to discern what it is. When I receive it, then I want to keep it and think about it and assess its flavour but forthwith it has gone.[7]

And so William turns to prayer: 'May every step that my soul takes be towards you, in you, and through you. And when my strength, which is nothing, fails, may my very weakness still pant for you.'[8]

A Way of Love

The way, then, to contemplative union with God is the way of love. So we need to understand what love is and how we grow in love. This was the next project William undertook: to explore and put in writing his thoughts *On the Nature and Dignity of Love*. It probably was not coincidental that at the same time Bernard was writing his treatise, *On Loving God*. Their literary endeavours would run parallel for much of their lives. For William, 'Love is a power of the soul, leading us by a kind of natural gravity to our place or destination. . . . We are always driven to this place by our own natural gravity, since we desire happiness, dream of happiness, and seek nothing but to be happy.'[9] This much was very clear to our abbot: 'Happy is that person – and no other – whose God is the Lord.'[10]

But, as William goes on to point out, 'having let natural teachings slip away, we need a teacher, a person who teaches about the happiness which we naturally seek through love, by admonishing where, how, in what territory, and by what path we are to seek'.[11]

William proposes to be such a teacher. He notes, however, that 'it is not to be taught as if it were something which no longer exists, but taught so that it may be purified and the way to be purified; taught so that it may increase and the way to increase; taught that it may be strengthened and the way to be strengthened'.[12]

For his teaching on love William chooses as his paradigm human growth:

> First of all, let us begin with the origins of love and then look at its development, as it were, through some successive stages until we come to a rich seniority which is full not of senile sadness but full of rich mercy. For as the various stages of life increase, so a lad develops into a young man, a young man into a mature man and a mature man into a senior. As there are changes in qualities, so there are changes in the names of each stage. In the same way, the will according to the development of its virtue grows into love, love into charity and charity into wisdom. . . .
>
> First of all, love's birthplace is God. There it is born, there nourished, there developed. . . . Love is given by God alone, and it endures in him, for it is due to no one else but him and for his sake.[13]

Ever the trinitarian theologian, William, in speaking of the origin of love, develops the trinitarian aspect:

When the Triune God created us in God's own image,
God formed in the human person a sort of likeness of
the Trinity wherein the image of the Creator-Trinity
was also to shine out. . . . Memory possesses and contains that to which we must strive; reason, that we must
strive; the will strives. These three (memory, reason
and will) are all one yet effectively three, just as in
the supreme Trinity there is one substance and three
persons.

This, then, is the birthplace of the will, its adoption,
its dignity, its nobility. When grace anticipates and
cooperates, the will begins to believe by its good assent
to Holy Spirit who is love and the Will of the Father and
Son. It begins to ardently will what God wills and what
memory and reason suggests it should will. By ardent
willing it becomes love. For love is nothing other than
the will ardently fixed on something good.[14]

He makes it clear that the whole of this process is a work
of grace. 'The will is filled with good when it is helped by
grace; with evil when left to itself; it is lacking in itself.'[15]

So we, by our very nature, by our creation and even
more so by our re-creation, are ordered to love. But as we
take our first steps on the way of love we are influenced
more by the spirit of fear, fear of the just punishments of
God. Led and nourished by grace, we are lead into love,
into a spirit of piety where we begin to love and reverence
God. As the child grows into the young man, the strength
and energy of youth are to be wholeheartedly devoted to
the development of the virtues. As William outlines the
ascetic life here for the youth, his dependence on the Rule
of Benedict is very much in evidence.

Youth is not yet very enlightened; William compares the young to the blind. They must work diligently as they are led. As they continue to mature, things begin to take on a new countenance for them:

> The better gifts, which they have laboured until now to emulate, themselves begin to appear to them in a more familiar way. The body, humbled by holy discipline, begins to pass from habit to the spontaneous service of the spirit. The inner countenance of the 'new man' begins to be re-newed day by day until it is unveiled to behold the good things of God.[16]

> The young, full of good hope, whose youth God begins to make happy, begin to grow into perfect persons, into the measure of the age of the fullness of Christ. For love now begins to be strengthened and illumined and to pass into charity: a love from God, in God, for God is charity.[17]

We have arrived at spiritual adulthood. We have become men and women of charity. William takes up St Paul's magnificent hymn in 1 Corinthians to speak of the characteristics of this new stage. He compares this new experience with what went before: it is using a cart instead of carrying things on our back like a mule; it is a royal banquet in comparison to rough country food. So here he warns of the danger of our being satisfied with this rich food and not continuing to strive for what is better. The Lord always has something better in store for us if we but keep seeking and striving. We are the ones who place limits, not God.

William also makes a very important distinction here. The deep orientation of our being to God through charity is just that, firm and stable and maintained by grace, and not a thing of feelings or emotion. He notes if we are 'occasionally wounded and weakened by the onslaught of sin, nevertheless we are not destroyed when the roots of our charity are very deeply fixed'.[18] And he offers the rather perceptive statement that 'Peter, when he sinned, did not lose charity, for he sinned more against truth than against charity when he lied by saying with his mouth that he did not belong to Jesus to whom he belonged wholly in his heart. Therefore charity's truth immediately washed away with tears falsehood's denial.'[19] Indeed, William goes even further: 'David, too, when he sinned did not lose charity. Rather, the charity in him was somehow stunned by the vehement sting of temptation. Charity in him was never abolished, but, as it were, somehow dazed; it woke up soon enough at the voice of the accusing prophet. He broke forth immediately in that confession of very ardent charity: "I have sinned against you, O Lord!"'[20] It is not easy for the mature Christian, rooted in charity, to break away from his Beloved. We belong to Christ even when we slip and fall. In all this William is inspired by St John: 'He says: He does not sin, because anyone who is born of God endures rather than commits sin.'[21]

The maturing adult develops the five senses of charity: physical love for parents which is as primitive as the sense of touch; social love for those who are one with us in the Church, sharing a certain taste for the things of God and being nourished by them; natural love, as natural as smell, which inclines us to solidarity with all humans; spiritual love which, through the hearing of the Word, obediently goes out even to love our enemies; and finally spiritual love or divine love, the most sublime, which leads us to the vision and experience of God.

William notes, too, that charity has, as it were, two eyes: reason and love. 'Reason cannot see God, except in what he is not, but love cannot bring itself to rest except in what he is.'[22] And he goes on: 'When they help one another – when reason teaches love and love enlightens reason – then they can do great things.'[23] But what can they do? Here William comes up with an answer which is standard among the Fathers and which we beginners find quite usually annoying: 'Just as anyone who progresses in this cannot progress and learn this except through his own experience, so also it can not be communicated to a person who has not had the experience.'[24] We are now truly in the 'School of Charity' where alone the experience of love teaches; Holy Spirit is the teacher:

> The Spirit of knowledge openly teaches us what to do and how to do it. The Spirit of fortitude confers the strength and virtues to accomplish this. The Spirit of counsel disposes us. And when we are free to be free in God, to cleave to God, we are made like to God through the piety of devotion and a unity of will.[25]

With this William goes on to describe life in the Spirit and how it is lived in Christian community, concluding: 'Is this not a celestial rather than an earthly paradise?'[26]

This is a lifetime's labour; we arrive finally at that venerable seniority when 'one is reputed to be venerable by the number not of years but of virtues; one aspires to the maturity of wisdom and to rest from labours'.[27] We want to leave behind the cares and preoccupations of this life. It is time to live the first commandment. Loving God with the whole heart or will, whole soul or love, whole strength or charity, we are ready to enjoy wisdom with the whole mind.

But the wisdom of God is not some abstract thing or a quality in our minds, it is God, the Son of God, Jesus Christ, incarnate Wisdom. William, like all the Cistercian Fathers, is ultimately Christocentric in his teaching. Here he develops with striking imagery Jesus' mediatorial role. And he stresses our need of the gift of understanding so that we might do most fruitful *lectio* and come to understand fully what the Scriptures seek to teach us about Christ.

He shares his own insight:

God the Son, the image of God, saw that both the angel and the human, who were made like unto him, that is, to the image of God, but not as he is, the Image of God, have perished through an inordinate appetite for his image and likeness. He then said: Misery alone lacks envy! Humans should be assisted as justice does not prohibit assisting them. Therefore I shall show myself to them as a man despised and the least of all men, a man of sorrows and knowing infirmity, that they may be zealous to imitate my humility. Through this they will come to the glory toward which they are hastening. Thus they may come to hear from me: 'Learn of me because I am meek and humble of heart, and you shall find rest for your souls.'[28]

The way of love and wisdom is the way of humility. This is the central insight of the Cistercian-Benedictine way to God.

Moreover, for William the way is consummated in the Eucharist:

> We have been satiated with the fruit of this work by the mediation of the Wisdom of God. Not only are we reconciled but we are even wise as well, for we savour what we eat. We eat and drink the Body and Blood of our Redeemer, the Heavenly Manna, the Bread of Angels, the Bread of Wisdom, and while eating it we are transformed into the nature of the food we eat. For to eat the Body of Christ is nothing other than to be made the body of Christ and the temple of Holy Spirit.[29]

Not long after writing this, William would devote a whole treatise, produced in response to a query from Rupert of Deutz, to *The Sacrament of the Altar*.

Finally, the journey is complete and we come to 'this transitus to life which wretched infidels call death.'[30]

> Yet, what do the faithful called it if not a passover? In bodily death, therefore, we die perfectly to the world that we may live perfectly in God. We have entered the place of the admirable tabernacle. We enter all the way into the house of God. . . . When all things go well according to order, gravity bears each to its proper place. The body returns to the earth from which it was taken, to be raised up and glorified in its own time, and the spirit returns to God who created it.[31]

This is the destination of those who set Jerusalem before their eyes at the beginning of their gladness, those whom Holy Spirit teaches about all things, those who wisely arrange ascents from virtue to virtue in their hearts until they see the God of gods in Zion, the God of gods, the beatitude of the blessed, the joy of those who rejoice well, the One Good, the highest Good of all. . . . We are led back to our beginning and are hidden in the hiddenness of the face of God.[32]

William ends his treatise with a very interesting paragraph, a sort of postscript. He tells us 'every wise climber must know that the stages of this ascent are not like the rungs of a ladder'.[33] We do not leave one behind as we ascend to the next. 'They all concur and work together, they lead, they follow. Often the first becomes the last and the last first.'[34] If we use the image of the ladder, this ladder is lying flat on the ground and we are on all the rungs at the same time.

The Lover

Having explored the way – love, William went on to explore those who do the loving: you and me – the lovers. His treatise *On the Body and Soul* finds its place at the beginning of a Cistercian tradition which was undoubtedly influenced by St Augustine's *Noverim me ut noverim Te*: Lord, may I know myself that I might know you. Fundamental to the Cistercian school was the theology of the image. Genesis tells us that we were made in the image and likeness of God. Bernard and the others are strong to affirm that while we lost the likeness and went off into a far country, a region of unlikeness, we ever retained the image. Our journey is to return home, to regain the divine likeness, which William finds essentially in a unity of spirit attained through love or a unity of wills.

Besides giving witness to Cistercian humanism, William's treatise *On the Body and Soul* has another significant message for us. Droll as we may find its medieval physiology, it was the latest and best available at that time, culled largely from the Islamic world. The openness that William shows us here in drawing from these scholars belonging to the menacing enemies of the Christian world challenges us to remain open today in our spiritual and human quest, a challenge very present in the documents of the Second Vatican Council. Today's Cistercians are significant participants in the interreligious dialogue. And Abbot Thomas Keating, as he developed his teaching on Centring Prayer published in his *Spiritual Journey*, has sought to use the best insights offered today by the behavioural sciences.

As William reminded us in his treatise on love, image though we are, we can do nothing good without grace. So to complete our understanding of ourselves, he produced one of his densest theological pieces, his *Commentary on the Epistle to the Romans*, which he dedicated to his friend Bernard. It is not surprising to find Bernard at the same time working on his important study *On Grace and Free Choice*.

With this groundwork done, William was ready to move towards what for many of the Cistercians was their most desired work, a commentary on God's own love song, the Song of Songs. In the early days of his abbacy, like so many abbots, William was laid low with some kind of debilitating illness that required long rest. It so happened that Bernard was also confined to the infirmary at that time. So he sent his brother Gerard to Saint Thierry to bring William to Clairvaux. For some six weeks the two abbots lay side by side in the infirmary, whiling away the hours by discoursing on the Song of Songs. Later there appeared a *Brief Commentary on the Song of Songs*, which has been attributed to William and has been believed to gather up the fruit of their sharings in the Clairvaux infirmary.

Certainly this sharing with Bernard whetted William's appetite. He now set to work to gather up all the texts on the Songs of Songs that he could find, first in the writings of St Ambrose, the great Bishop of Milan, who provided the Cistercians and the Church in general with many of the hymns used at the canonical hours. Then he went on to the Western Father who perhaps had the greatest influence on the early Cistercians, Pope Gregory the Great, the author of the life of St Benedict. These two rich collections of excerpts further fuelled William's interest in the Song.

Even while he devoted himself to this ever-deeper understanding of the spiritual journey, William was carrying out the charge given to him by Bernard when he wanted to move to Clairvaux: to foster renewal among the Benedictines. Finally in 1132 all the Benedictine abbots of his region gathered at Rheims. Their *Letter to Cardinal Matthew*, precisely laying out their renewal programme, has been considered to be primarily the work of William. With this accomplished, William felt he had fulfilled his mandate and could now retire to the Cistercian life. Since Bernard was not in accord with this judgement, while the holy abbot was at Rome William resigned his office at

Saint Thierry and entered the nearby Cistercian abbey of Signy.

The Meditations

It seems one of the first tasks William set himself to with his new found leisure was to gather up some of his notes and prepare a treatise to help the young to learn to pray. Later editors divided this somewhat rambling work into twelve distinct meditations according to the twelve long paragraphs discovered in William's manuscript. A short separate meditation was found later to give us a thirteenth.

William takes one Scripture text after another and develops the insight he has received from it. This might suggest to us the best way to use the *Meditations*: to take the Scripture texts one by one and absorb the insight following each one. The basic text is that from William's favourite Psalm: 'Seek the face of God.'[35] If anything provides a unifying theme in this work, this is it. Certainly this is not surprising for a son of the saint who set as the primary requirement for a monk that 'he truly seek God'.[36] William makes it a very personal encounter. Here he is in all his misery and there is God in all his infinite perfection. How is the gap to be bridged? The answer lies in Christ who is the open door into heaven, into the divine presence.

The first meditation stands out as one of the most carefully crafted of the twelve. Considering that William and Bernard had worked on treatises concerning human free will and the operation of divine grace with its prescience or predestination, the question was there for William. If election 'is not of the person who wills, nor of the person who runs, but of God who shows mercy'[37] then, to use the questions from the Epistle to the Romans, 'Why does God find fault? For who can resist God's will?'[38]

William's attitude in the face of the mystery is powerfully expressed:

> Have mercy on us, Lord, have mercy! You are the potter, we are the clay. . . . Cleanse our reins and our hearts by the fire of your Holy Spirit and establish the work you have wrought in us. . . . We were created for you by yourself and towards you our face is set.[39]

After many fine distinctions, William contents himself with a response taken almost word for word from St Augustine: 'Why one should be taken into grace and another rejected, is a question you had best not ask, unless you wish to go astray.'[40]

I think, though, that young people are apt to find that William's eleventh meditation speaks to them more significantly than this exploration of predestination. This meditation harks back to the time when William was still abbot at Saint Thierry and was trying to decide whether he could lay down his abbatial charge and seek a more contemplative life among the Cistercians, or whether the Lord wanted him to continue to serve.

William had wholly turned towards the Lord:

> 'Turn us again, O God of hosts: show your face, and we shall be saved.' Thanks to your gift of grace, O Lord, my heart's face is not turned to fleshly things, for you have put all these behind my back, together with the world and all that goes with it.[41]

Now he is confronted with the practical question: How is he to live this? And where?

> Command what you will, and make me understand your command. As you have given me the will to do it, so also give the power; and in me and concerning me your whole will shall be done. I have set my will to do your will, O God, and I embrace with all my heart your law in your commands. . . . But I am groping in the noonday like a blind person now, in whatever direction I decide to move, I go in fear of pitfalls and destruction. And, like a blind man I am told to go hither and thither, by this way or by that, while I myself, just like a sightless person, do not know in what direction I am travelling, nor by what road I go.[42]

Inspired by the text in Hebrews which speaks of the Word of God as 'dividing asunder the soul and the spirit, the joints and the marrow, discerning the thoughts and intentions of the heart',[43] William presents his struggle as a dramatic debate among these within him. Anyone who has really struggled with a decision can readily identify with this inner struggle so dramatically presented. In presenting the importance of a centred life, it is the marrow, the deepest part of us, that sets forth the principles by which the question is to be decided:

> Let us review our affections and actions. Let our affections be set on the centre of truth, and then the outward action will correspond thereto, as the circumference to the centre. Every affection is indeed owed to God. When he is adhered to faithfully, whenever the circle of

activity revolves, it cannot err from the right but meets itself truly, so that its radius is of equal length at every point. There can be a point without a circle, but in no way can a circle be drawn without a central point.

Affection is sufficient if circumstances do not demand action or the possibility of acting is lacking. But when the demands of love require action, true charity owes it to God or to a neighbour as the case may be; if necessity does not require it, the love of truth makes it our duty to hold ourselves at leisure for itself. And as we always owe our entire affection to God, so also, when we are at leisure, we owe our whole activity to God. And when a neighbour's need does not require it, we who divert a part of our affection or activity from God commit a sacrilege. But when necessity does require us to act we must not be so eager to perform it that we fail to take stock of our own ability to do it. The centre of truth must be consulted as to whether we have the ability or not. If we have not, and yet presume to act, we are not cleaving to this centre, and so we destroy the perfection of the circumference. For there are people who have no love for cleaving to the point of stability; they always want to be circling around outside. . . .

Let us from whom action is urgently demanded, if indeed we can do so, fix our attention on the truth, and not refuse to do the active service. If the truth, when it has been consulted, tells us we are unequal to the task and no fit person for it, then let us fix our soul in stillness on the stability of truth, lest, being as it were on the rim of the wheel, we be sent over the precipice of error.[44]

Spirit confirms this: 'This is indeed the marrow and centre of the truth. . . .'[45] And Soul adds: 'This is how the matter stands.'[46] With this, William concludes the discussion with his own affirmation: 'Let us cry with our whole heart and mind: "Jesus, Son of David, have mercy on me!"'[47]

In Meditation 12 William moves to his conclusion and it is indeed for him a commencement, a new beginning: 'I come to you today as one whose whole past life is dead so that in you, O Fountain of New Life, I may begin again. If I have done any good things, they are yours. To you I hand them over; do you return them to me in your own good time. The bad things that I have committed are my own. . . . O that a suitable repentance may efface them from your remembrance.'[48] He moves ahead with great confidence, concretely described: 'I am committing myself with complete trust into your hands, of which so often I have had experience. When one of your hands strikes me, the other caresses and when one knocks me down, the other catches me so that I am not bruised.'[49] And he gives expression to his deepest desire: 'If only I might be found fully worthy to behold the face of your love, to walk openly in its light and to enjoy its pleasures, I would not mind at all how I gave myself for it, either in death or life.'[50]

With this William sums up the journey of love:

When in my meditation the fire kindles and I try to find out what I have and what I lack, asking your help in the matter I begin to make a staircase for myself, by which I may ascend to you. The steps of it that I set up for myself in my heart are these: first, a great will is needed, then an enlightened will, and thirdly, a will upon which love has laid its hand. Everyone who mounts to you needs first this great will, great as he can make it. He also needs a will enlightened by your gift and moved in your own way – a will that is as great as you created it, enlightened as far as you have made it worthy to receive your light and moved according to the form that you have given it.[51]

And he goes on to conclude his treatise with a prayer:

Come, therefore, come, O holy Love; come, O sacred Fire! Burn up the concupiscences of our reins and our hearts. Hide your thoughts as you will, to furnish more abundantly the rule of humility for your revealing flame. Manifest them when you will, to manifest the glory of a good conscience and the riches it has in its house. Manifest those riches, Lord, to make the zealous to keep them; Hide them from me, lest I be led rashly to squander them, until such time as he who has begun the good work shall also perfect it, he who lives and reigns through all the ages of ages.[52]

Love's Song

With his past put in order and holy leisure assured him, William is now ready to embark upon the task he has longed for, to study and comment on God's great love song. He approaches his task with his usual humility and deference towards his friend, Bernard, who in his turn is also embarking upon his own monumental collection of sermons on this Song of Songs: 'We do not presume to treat of those deeper mysteries the Song of Songs contains

with regard to Christ and the Church; but restraining ourselves within ourselves and measuring ourselves by ourselves, in the poverty of our understanding we shall (as
anyone may venture to do) touch lightly on a certain
moral sense apropos of Bridegroom and bride, Christ and
Christian soul.'[53]

William makes it clear what is his intent in undertaking
this *Exposition on the Song of Songs*: 'Far be it from the
heart and intention of your poor servant to seek and envi-
sion in this study any purpose but one – that, by seeing
your splendour and experiencing your charity, my conscience may be enlightened in you and my soul purified by
your influence; and that by pondering these songs which
pertain to you and impart your delightful taste and sweet
perfume, I may savour your taste and perceive your
fragrance and my life may be wholly moulded in you and
by your influence.'[54]

Seeking to speak about what is ultimately beyond the
grasp of reason, and, using the rich imagery provided by
the Song of Songs, he circles around, adding description to
description of the journey into the experience of God,
drawing us in ever more by the beauty of his discourse
towards

> that wonderful union and mutual enjoyment – of sweet-
> ness and of joy incomprehensible and inconceivable
> even for those in whom it takes place – between us and
> God, the created spirit and the Uncreated. . . . By this
> union we become one spirit with God not by that eter-
> nal kiss and perfect union, which is nothing else than
> the unity of the Father and the Son of God, their Kiss,
> their Embrace, their Love, their Goodness, but by a

certain remote imitation of that kiss and perfection and
a certain likeness of that union and likeness. For by the
action of Holy Spirit, our spirit and a sense of enlightened love sometimes fleetingly attain to it. Then that
something, what ever it is – something loved rather than
thought and tasted rather than understood – grows
sweet and ravishes the lover. And for a moment, for an
hour, this affects us and shapes our efforts until it seems
to us that no longer in hope but in quasi-reality we see
with our eyes and hold and handle with our hands, by a
sort of evidence of experiential faith, the very substance
of things to be hoped for of the Word of Life.[55]

It is here, when he has more experience than he had
when he wrote *On Contemplating God*, that William
explores the contemplative experience: 'In contemplation
of God where love is chiefly operative, reason passes into
love and is transformed into a certain spiritual and divine
understanding which transcends and absorbs all reason.'[56]
Contemplation has two eyes, 'one searches human things
according to knowledge; the other, divine things according
to wisdom'.[57] The key to this wisdom and the contemplation of the Divine is that divine action which he calls illuminating grace. When under the influence of this grace
'humble love turns towards God more ardently, it is conformed to God towards whom it turns; because as it turns
it is given by God an aptitude for such conformity. And
since we are made in the likeness of our Maker, we
become attracted to God; that is, we become one spirit
with God, beautiful in God's beauty, good in God's goodness; and this takes place in proportion to the strength of
our faith, the light of our understanding and the measure

of our love. We are then in God, by grace, what God is by nature.'[58]

He defines the place of activity in the journey of the contemplative: 'No less blessed is the conscience that leaves the joy of this interior sweetness to perform some need to work at the command of charity, yet, no matter where it has been, always has the way prepared for its return home. . . . We must always leave behind something of ourselves which will safely keep our place for us; to which the part of us forced to go forth must always cling by a strong bond of love. . . . Let not the force of outward obligations ever succeed in withdrawing our whole soul from the enthralment of inward sweetness.'[59] The contemplative 'cannot but love goodness in others' for 'anyone who truly loves God, loves and embraces love wherever one finds it'.[60] Thus it happens that we come to love our neighbour as ourselves and even more, for we are painfully conscious of our own limitations and failures and more readily see the goodness in our neighbours without perceiving their inner faults.[61] After this William explores at length the whole ordering of charity in us.[62]

As one would expect from a Cistercian, William emphasizes the role of humility, and here his Christo-centrism shines forth.[63] And, of course, he also speaks of our joy.[64]

Lectio is also a part of the programme, and we find a surprising development in William's thinking:

'Voice' is better here than 'word', . . . The voice that pronounces the word is the efficacious power of the Divinity, which breaks the cedars of Lebanon, the arro-gant ways of human wisdom and worldly pride. This voice is not heard except in the secrecy of silence; it takes effect only in a pure heart. . . . To her who is a bride the Word of God utters himself and his Father, in the Spirit of his mouth. . . . And this same voice becomes both the voice of the Bridegroom to the bride and the voice in the bride to the Bridegroom, in the joy of mutual union and enjoyment in which they constantly converse and answer one another. It is the goodness of him who gives and the love of her who receives.[65]

Several times in the course of his exposition William stops to summarize the journey he is tracing out, actually noting that he is tracing out the beginning journey of the novice:

Here we have the entire sequence: hope hastens, desire becomes a crucifixion, wisdom sets all in order, love speeds forward, and grace is there to meet; until finally, at the end of the Song, the grief of the soul's desire is turned into the joy of experience, the weariness of delay being at last exchanged for mutual union.[66]

William did not complete his *Exposition*. In fact he only reached the third chapter of the Song. But the last paragraph that he wrote seems to be an apt conclusion:

For we must finally accomplish our journey where we shall no longer read except in the Book of Truth where Eternal Wisdom shall be given instead of meditation; vision, instead of consolation; the face to face, instead of the glass and the original. But this is far beyond you, since it is the state of the future life and eternal beatitude, which exceeds and transcends all weakness. But only a little beyond you is the state of devotion in which the Bridegroom sometimes helps the weakness of his bride, whoever she is, that she may gain a foretaste of these things. ... The state of the good soul, attained through progress in virtue, is free from the lower darkness and illuminated at closer range by the splendour from above.[67]

A Life of Faith

As he worked on the *Exposition* William's holy leisure was beginning to be disturbed by the fact that others were becoming upset. This monk who always had a very special concern for the young, was not happy to see the faith of the young men entering Signy greatly agitated by the unbridled speculation of the brilliant monk, Abelard. Study showed this schoolmaster's writings to be seeded with errors. William called forth his powerful friend, Bernard, to respond to the famous Paris lecturer while he set his pen to work to help the infected youths. First he produced a very clear and practical treatise on faith itself: the *Mirror of Faith*, and then went on to lay out the primary objects of that faith in his rather more dense *Enigma of Faith*.

For William faith gives birth to hope and finds its full expression and enjoyment in the experience of love. Its goal is union with God. Thus his first chapters in the *Mirror of Faith* are about the three theological virtues, and the last are about the goal, the presence of the Spirit and union. In between, in good Benedictine fashion, he

emphasizes the importance of humility for the possession
and practice of this virtue[68] and explores the difficult question of the relationship of faith to understanding. In this
eminently practical and useful little treatise he does speak
of the object of faith but it is in what he refers to as the
'second book', the *Enigma of Faith*, that he delves into
faith's most proper object, the most holy Trinity.

> Perfection in this life is nothing other than forget-
> ting entirely, by mean of faith, hope and charity, those
> things that are behind and pushing on to those that are
> ahead. . . . In the likeness of the Most Blessed Trinity,
> faith begets hope and charity proceeds from both, that
> is, from faith and from hope, for one cannot help but
> love what one believes in and hopes for.[69]

> Faith is indeed the first step forward to God.'[70]

By a wonderful play on words William reminds us 'we
do not have a right faith about faith if we do not faithfully
understand, above all, whose gift it is. Faith has an element of free will but of a will freed by grace. . . . By God's
inspiration we make a voluntary assent of the mind to
those things which concern God . . . and that is faith.'[71]
Again we find him struggling with the challenge of grace
and free will, the mystery of predestination.

He summarizes the object and activity of faith:

> Anyone who believes ought to know what he believes,
> who is the author of it and who is teaching it, that he
> may believe what he believes. Anyone who is really a
> faithful believer and of good will concerning the faith

never picks out from among the matters of faith what one wants to believe, but without any retraction or hesitation one believes whatever divine authority has indicated must be believed. Nor do we, by devising for ourselves new beliefs, savour those things which are, as it were, more agreeable to our physical sensitivities. Rather we always try to savour those things that are true. We apply our reason to them and study the doctrine about them. Nor do we hesitate over them by judging them with human reason, but hold them as certain by clinging to them in faith and love.[72]

For our consolation, though, he notes:

Even some among the ranks of the faithful stumble quite often. Although they do not stumble enough to fall. ... Even minds quite fervent in religion, but still rather immature in the faith often undergo temptations about faith that come not by assailing them openly but by attacking them as if from the side and by plucking at the garment of faith from behind. They do not say: yes, yes, no, no; but whisper: maybe, maybe! Maybe it is so, they say; maybe it is not! Maybe it is otherwise; maybe it is otherwise than written – on account of something that was not written down. ... Although the garment of faith is found intact, it still feels plucked and battered.[73]

And William goes on to give a lot of good practical advice for overcoming temptation[74] as well as for building up faith.[75]

In fact, there seems to be a reason which attacks and a reason which defends faith. The first one thinks of things in an animal or physical way, the other is spiritual and discerns all things spiritually. The one is, as it were, hesitant about unknown things, the other submits everything to authority. Moreover, it can hardly bear that any doubt should arise in any part of itself. It does not give doubtful assent to anything coming from divine authority and from faith unfeigned. But what does the spirit do, once it believes in God? It reads the Gospels for itself, the words as well as the miracles of the Lord, and in all of them it venerates and adores the sacred vestiges of truth. When its faith is challenged, it says: You are the Christ, the Son of God.[76]

With this distinction between the animal soul and the spiritual soul, William is preparing the way for his ultimate synthesis in the _Golden Epistle_. It all leads to what he calls, _unitas spiritus_, unity of spirit:

Holy Spirit who is the substantial will of the Father and the Son so attaches the will of a person to herself that the soul, loving God and, by loving, having an experiential sense of God, will be unexpectedly and entirely transformed, not into the nature of the divinity certainly, but into a kind of blessedness beyond the human form yet short of the divine, in the joy of illuminating grace and the sense of an enlightened conscience. This is so true that our spirit which before had scarcely been able to say in Holy Spirit: Jesus is Lord, now amid the sons and daughters of adoption, cries out: _Abba_, Father![77]

For William this 'unity of spirit' is not an individualistic thing: 'It is not one person only but many persons who have one heart and one soul in Holy Spirit as a result of the sharing of this supreme charity at the source of which is the unity of the Trinity.'[78]

This wonderful and wonderfully rich little treatise includes a very meaty presentation of sacramental theology,[79] the centrality of Christ, Sacrament and Mediator,[80] and in what is for William a rather unique Marian paragraph, the modelling of Mary, the faithful one.[81] We have to smile when in the last paragraph of his treatise William says: 'Would that we understood what we are saying. . . . We throw words around; we are carried away with words and we are held back from what cannot be expressed by any words. And yet, nothing can be said except in words.'[82] It is in the realization of the poverty of our words that he makes his plea for a wordless, contemplative prayer, free from our poor concepts:

It advances the person advancing no little if that person accepts nothing in God's place which is not God himself, so that this faithful mind shuts out and rejects anything physical or localized which occurs to it or anything exhibiting a form of quality or dimension of quantity. Let the mind reflect on truth itself insofar as it can and let it recognize it with absolute certitude and love it. It discerns that this truth truly exists from the fact that it loves even a truth not reflected upon. This truth is God, who is what he is and from whom and through whom and in whom is all that is. . . .

All the acts or words of the Word of God are for us therefore one word. Everything about him which we

read, we hear, we see, we speak, we meditate on, either
by provoking love or inculcating fear, call us to the
One, sends us to the One of whom many things are said
and nothing is said, because we do not come to that
which is unless he who is sought runs to us and shines
his face upon us. May he shine his face upon us that in
the light of his face we may know how we are going.[83]

The *Enigma of Faith* is William's most speculative
work. He exercises his intellect and ours to the full in the
face of the supreme mystery: how God is one and three.
But even here, the Cistercian, the man of heart, wins out
as devotion repeatedly breaks through in prayer. After
investigating 'the exterior reasoning of the faith concerning the Trinity and its external expression'[84] and explor-
ing the complex understandings of the divine names,[85]
William proceeds 'with fear and trembling' to the contemplation of the Mystery. Holy Spirit, who has been given to
us, 'teaching us to pray as we ought and drawing us to
God and rendering us pleasing and able to be heard, illu-
mines our intellect and shapes our disposition. The Spirit
creates and brings to perfection.'[86] It will be in the third
part of his magnificent synthesis, his *Letter to the Brothers
of Mount Dieu*, the *Golden Epistle*, that William will fully
develop what he opens out here very briefly.

A Golden Synthesis

What led William to spend some time at the Charterhouse
recently founded in the neighbourhood of his monastery,
we do not know. It was undoubtedly a time of refreshment and peace for him as well as an encouragement for

the Carthusian brethren, like the early Cistercians, who were being accused of introducing 'novelties' into the age-old monastic traditions. In any case, in gratitude to these monks of Mont Dieu, William sent an extensive letter which he said was meant primarily for the benefit of 'the younger brethren and the novices'.[87] The fairly brief prefatory letter is in itself most precious for it gives us a literary autobiography of the author. William's extensive letter which follows has rightly been called the *Golden Epistle*. It is a clear, well-developed synthesis of the whole of his ascetical and mystical theology immediately and directly applied to life with great practicality.

Basically William adopts the classical three stages of the spiritual journey but creatively names them animal, rational and spiritual, using for the soul three distinct Latin words: *anima* (the feminine soul), *animus* (the virile soul) and *spiritus* (the soul as it enters into union with the Divine Spirit).

> There are the beginners, those who are making progress and the perfect. The state of the beginners may be called 'animal', the state of those who are making progress 'rational' and the state of the perfect 'spiritual'.[88]

> The first state is concerned with the body, the second with the soul, the third finds rest only in God. Each of them makes progress after its own fashion and each of them has a certain measure of perfection proper to itself.[89]

> The beginning of good in the animal way of life is perfect obedience; progress for it is to gain control of the body and bring it into subjection; perfection for it is

when the habitual exercise of virtue has become a pleasure. The beginning of the rational state is to understand what is set before it by the teaching of the faith;
progress is a life lived in accordance with that teaching;
perfection is when the judgement of the reason passes
into a spiritual perfection. The perfection of the rational
state is the beginning of the spiritual state; progress in it
is to look upon God's glory with face uncovered; and its
perfection is to be transformed into the same likeness,
borrowing glory from that glory, enabled by the spirit
of the Lord.[90]

Given the audience to whom William was primarily
directing his letter, it is not surprising to find his treatment
of the animal state much longer and more detailed than
that of the last two states. With St Paul he counsels the
beginners to 'offer up their bodies as a living sacrifice',[91]
not be 'overhasty and inquisitive in examining the things
of the spirit and of God'[92] and 'to deaden in accord with
reason those passions which belong to the earth'.[93] 'The
servants of God should never be idle, although they are at
leisure to devote themselves to God.'[94] They have a rule of
life that allots to every hour its due exercise:[95] prayer and
the Eucharist, lectio, examen (the daily practice when
monastics examine their response to the Lord in their daily
activities), work and physical exercises. With ascetical practice 'we do not lose our pleasures, we only transfer them
from the body to the soul, from the senses to the spirit'.[96]

After giving the beginners a word of hope:

When they have reached the end of this animal or
human stage, if they do not look back, if they press on

faithfully to what lies before them, they will quickly arrive at that divine state in which they will begin to possess as they are possessed and to know as they are known. This, however, is a task that is not completed in a moment, at a person's conversion, nor in a single day: it demands a long time and much hard work, much sweat; it depends on God's mercy and grace and on our will and alacrity.[97]

William goes on to give richly detailed advice in regard to each of the exercises, guarding always his very balanced humanism. Take for example his words about fasting and sleep:

If you eat, let your sobriety lend its adornment to a table which is already sparing. And when you eat do not give yourself wholly to the business of eating. While the body is securing its refreshment let not the mind wholly neglect its own but dwell upon and as it were digest something that it recalls of the Lord's sweetness or a passage from the Scriptures that will feed it as it meditates upon it or at least remembers it. The bodily need itself should be satisfied not in a worldly or carnal way but as befits a Christian and is becoming to God's servant. Even from the point of view of health, the more becoming and orderly the manner of eating, the easier and more wholesome is the process of digestion.

Watch must be kept then on the manner and the time of eating, on the quality and quantity of the food; all of superfluity and seasonings that only adulterate food should be shunned.

Watch must be kept on the manner, so that we eaters

do not pour out our souls over everything we eat; watch on the time, lest the hour be anticipated; on the quality, which should be that of the common food except when obvious infirmity demands something better. As regards seasoning let it be enough, I beg, that our food be edible, not also such as to provoke appetite or tickle the palate. Appetite contains enough disorder of itself; it can scarcely or not at all satisfy its needs without the accompaniment of some enjoyment and if it begins to receive stimulants from those who have declared an unending war on its enticements, it is two against one and temperance is endangered.

The same applies to sleep as has been said about food. Take care, servant of God, as far as you can, never to give yourself wholly to sleep, lest your sleep be not the rest of a weary person but the entombment of a stifled body; not the refreshment but the extinction of your spirit. Sleep is something of which to be watchful. . . .

Accordingly when you go to sleep always take with you in your memory or your thoughts something that will enable you to fall asleep peacefully and sometimes even help you to dream; something also that will come to mind when you wake up and renew anew the previous day's purpose. In this way light will be shed on the night for you and it will be as the day, and the night will be your illumination in your delights. You'll fall asleep peacefully, you will rest in tranquillity, you wake up easily and when you rise you'll have no difficulty in returning with your wits about you to do what you have not wholly laid aside.

For temperate food and moderation of the senses are followed by undisturbed sleep. . . . From temperate sleep it is easy after a suitable period of repose to recall the senses both of body and of mind, rousing them and setting them to work like the servants of a well-ordered household to do whatever tasks are required by the spirit. Such sleep at the right time and in the right manner is not to be scorned.[98]

William breaks off to speak to some community concerns: vocations, poverty, self-support. And then he returns to the subject of prayer, adding a rich section. Here are a few of his pithy insights:

Prayer is affection in a person who clings to God, a confident and devout conversation, a state in which the enlightened enjoys God as long as it is permitted.[99]

When we make petition God indeed approves our good will but God follows God's own better judgement and enables the one who makes petition in the right spirit to acquiesce in God's will.[100]

When it is a question of petition prayer should be made devoutly and with faith but without obstinate persistence, since it is not we but our Father who is in heaven who knows what we need in these temporal things.[101]

Moving on to a consideration of the remaining two stages, the rational and the spiritual, William points out that they really come together. His treatment of the rational state is largely an abstract consideration of the human components involved: reason, vices and virtues, will and thought. Repeated descriptive definitions are offered, for example:

Virtue is a willing assent to good.
Virtue is a certain balance of life, conforming to reason all things.
Virtue is the use of free will according to the judgement of reason.
Virtue is a certain humility, a certain patience.
Virtue is nothing other than the use of free will in accordance with the judgement of reason.[102]

When he comes to write of the spiritual state it is largely a celebration of what is attained.

When the object of thought is God and the things which relate to God, and will reaches the stage at which it becomes love, Holy Spirit, the Spirit of Life, at once infuses herself by way of love and gives life to everything, lending her assistance in prayer, in meditation or in study to our weakness. Immediately the memory becomes wisdom and tastes with relish the good things of the Lord, while the thoughts to which they give rise are brought to the intellect to be formed into affections. The understanding of the one thinking becomes a contemplation of one loving and it shapes it into certain experiences of spiritual or divine sweetness, which it brings before the gaze of the spirit so that the spirit rejoices in them.[103]

The will is now something more than will; it is love, dilection, charity and unity of spirit. For such is the way in which God is to be loved. 'Love' is a strong inclination of the will toward God, 'dilection' is a clinging to God or union with God; 'charity' is the enjoyment of

God. But 'unity of spirit' with God for those of us who
have our hearts raised on high is the term of the will's
progress toward God. No longer do we merely desire
what God desires, not only do we love God, but we are
perfect in our love so that we can will only what God
wills.[104]

William goes on to describe more fully this state which
he sees as the ultimate goal of our life:

It is called unity of spirit not only because Holy Spirit
brings it about or inclines our spirit to it, but because it
is Holy Spirit herself, the God who is charity. Holy
Spirit who is the love of Father and Son, their Unity,
Sweetness, Good, Kiss, Embrace and whatever else they
can have in common in that supreme unity of truth and
truth of unity, becomes for us in regard to God in the
manner appropriate to us what she is for the Son in
regard to the Father or for the Father in regard to the
Son through unity of substance. This soul in its happiness finds itself standing midway in the Embrace and the
Kiss of Father and Son. In a manner which exceeds
description and thought, the servant of God is found
worthy to be, not God but what God is, that is to say
we become through grace what God is by nature.[105]

He then, as it were, sings a hymn of praise in honour of
Holy Spirit:

Holy Spirit is the almighty Artificer
    who creates our good will in regard to God,
    who inclines God to be merciful to us,

who shapes our desire,
who gives strength,
who ensures the prosperity of undertakings,
who conducts all things powerfully
and discloses everything sweetly.

Holy spirit it is who gives life to our spirit and holds it
    together . . .
Others may teach how to seek God and angels how to
    adore God,
but Holy Spirit alone teaches how to find God,
                                possess God,
                                enjoy God.
Holy Spirit is the anxious quest of those who truly
    seek,
Holy Spirit is the devotion of those who adore in spirit
    and in truth.
Holy Spirit is the wisdom of those who find,
            the love of those who possess,
            the gladness of those who enjoy.[106]

Nonetheless, William tells us that whatever Holy Spirit bestows upon us here by way 'of the vision and the knowledge of God' is as in a mirror and an enigma, 'as far removed from the vision and the knowledge that is to be in the future as faith is from vision or time from eternity'.[107] If God does give us a quickly passing glimpse of the light of the divine countenance insofar as we can grasp it here, it is to make us realize to some extent what we lack and to make us more eager to attain to that purity of heart which will make us worthy one day to truly see the face of God.

Even when he seems to be totally taken up into the

Transcendent, William, in the Christocentricism of the Cistercians, turns to the incarnate God, Christ our Lord:

It is impossible indeed for the supreme Good to be seen and not loved or not to be loved to the full extent to which vision of it has been granted. So eventually love arrives at some likeness of that love which made God like to us by accepting the humiliation of our human lot in order that we might be made like to God by receiving the glorification of communion in the divine life. Then indeed it is sweet for us to be abased together with supreme Majesty, to become poor together with the Son of God, to be conformed to the divine Wisdom, to make our own the mind which is in Christ Jesus our Lord.

For here there is wisdom with devotion, love with fear, exultation with trembling, when God is thought of and understood as brought down onto death, the death of the cross, to the end that we might be exalted to the likeness of the Godhead. From here there flows the rushing stream that gladdens God's City, the remembrance of his astounding sweetness in the understanding and consideration of the benefits he has conferred on us.[108]

As William now draws near to the end of his treatise he summarizes the journey:

When reason in conformity with wisdom forms a conscience and draws up a rule of life, in the lower kinds of knowledge it avails itself of nature's services and resources, in reasonings and the things of reason it follows the rule it has laid down, in the acquisition of

virtues it obeys its conscience. Thus making progress by
means of lower things, finding assistance in higher
things, continuing on its way toward what is right it
brings into play the judgement of reason, the assent of
the will, the inclination of the mind and external activity
and so hastens to arrive at liberty and unity of spirit, in
order that, as has already been said often, the person of
faith may become one spirit with God. . . . And this is
our perfection in this life.[109]

And once again, before he brings this magnificent letter to
a close, William seeks to find some words to express 'what
is better thought than spoken of':

God is to be attained by faith and, to the extent that
      Holy Spirit helps our weakness, by thought as
   Eternal Life, living and bestowing life,
   the Unchangeable, immutably making all changeable
      things,
   the Intelligent, creating all understanding and every
      intellectual being,
   Wisdom, the source of all wisdom,
   the Truth that stands fast without any swearing,
   the Source of all truth,
   the Eternal principal containing all things that
      exist in time.[110]

'We are wholly unequal to the task of conceiving this
reality. . .'[111]

3

THE WAY OF FRIENDSHIP
Aelred of Rievaulx

Aelred was in one sense on the fringes of the great Cistercian movement. In fact he was at the centre of another albeit subordinate circle of Cistercian life. Rievaulx, if not the first Cistercian foundation in the Islands, was without doubt the most important. It sprang directly from Clairvaux and St Bernard; its first abbot was Bernard's own secretary. Aelred was its third and most important abbot, directed and guided by Bernard himself.

Aelred was not a product of the schools but still enjoyed a rich ecclesiastical (his father was a relatively important hierarch) and social formation, enjoying all the benefits of the royal court of Scotland. He didn't come to the cloister a saint but he wholeheartedly set himself in that direction and made great strides. After only eight years of Cistercian life he was not only appointed novice master and then abbot but he was commanded by Bernard to write a manual for novices of the Order. If Citeaux is a *schola caritatis*, a school of charity, then Aelred's *Mirror of Charity* is a basic textbook for that school. Here we will find traced out for us the basic lineaments of the way of love.

But Aelred didn't stop there. Inspired by Bernard's life as well as his own attraction, Aelred sought to live that love to the full, and this meant friendship – friendship with God and with one's fellows. And, as Aelred brings out in the literary device he uses, spiritual friendship is the product of living the *Mirror of Charity* through several decades.

Aelred was in his own wonderful and most beautiful way a great contemplative. He knew the Sabbath of heavenly contemplation. But he was also a Christian humanist through and through. 'Christ Love', to use Aelred's term, was ever at the centre of his life. Christ in all humanness ever called forth the tender devotion of this most loving of *abba*s – the abbot who was friend.

This strong incarnationalism wedded to his noble background never allowed Aelred to divorce himself from the political powers of his time. In his 'political' writings he gives guidance to an authentic Christian concern for the kings of this world, how we ought to render unto Ceasar the things that are Ceasar's

Aelred entered upon the Cistercian way when Bernard was already clearly in his ascendancy (1134). Their points of direct contact were few but significant. Aelred lived to see the other Cistercian evangelists pass. He had the riches not only of Bernard's *Sermons on the Song of Songs* but also of his great synthesis in the *De consideratione* and William's abundant legacy in the *Golden Epistle*. He doesn't seem to have captured all their psychological insight. He was not so much at home with Bernard's rich allegorization. He was closer to Guerric of Igny's practical everyday wisdom that pointed to the fullest union with God even for the ordinary person. But he saw it flowering in the rich garden of a community of friends, companions entering together into the divine embrace.

A Novice's Manual

Aelred's first work, not unlike William's first Cistercian undertaking, the *Meditations*, is in part a compilation of notes he had been making over the years. But it is also like William's ultimate work, a synthesis of what would continue to be his teaching. To justify so young a monk – he had been less than a decade in the Order, a man in his early thirties – undertaking such an ambitious work, Aelred sets forth the mandate of Bernard of Clairvaux, who, as abbot of the monastery from which the founding monks of Rievaulx came, continued to exercise a certain jurisdiction as Father Immediate (to use the Cistercian term).

In this three-part work, most properly the first book is the 'mirror', reflecting for us the true nature of charity. The second book tells us more how to grow in this central virtue. And the third sets forth its fulfilment in the enjoyment of the threefold Sabbath.

Aelred begins with a prayer that gives us a sense of this beautiful man and enables him with the poetry of love to tell us what love is:

Let your voice sound in my ears, good Jesus, so that my heart may learn how to love you, my mind how to love you, the inmost being of my soul how to love you. Let the inmost core of my heart embrace you, my one and only true good, my dear and delightful joy. But, my God, what is love? Unless I am mistaken, love is a wonderful delight of the spirit: all the more attractive because more chaste, all the more gentle because more guileless and all the more enjoyable because more ample. It is the heart's palate which tastes that you are sweet, the heart's eye which sees that you are good. The heart is the place capable of receiving you, great as you are. Someone who loves you grasps you. The more one loves the more one grasps because you yourself are love, you are charity. This is the abundance of your house, by which your beloved ones will become so inebriated that, quitting themselves, they will pass into you. And how else, O Lord, but by loving you and this with all their being.

I pray you, Lord, let but a drop of your surpassing sweetness fall upon my soul, that by it the bread of my bitterness may become sweet. In experiencing a drop of this may I have a foretaste of what to desire, what to long for, what to sigh for here on my pilgrimage. In my hunger let me have a foretaste, in my thirst let me drink. For those who eat you will still hunger and those who drink you will still thirst. Yet they shall be filled when your glory appears and when will be manifest the abundance of your sweetness that you reserve for those who fear you and disclose only to those who love you.[1]

Aelred then goes on to set forth the 'image' theology common to the Cistercian school. Created in the image of the Creator to share in God's happiness, we withdrew from God and sought an illusive happiness in ourselves.

Made in the image of its Creator, the rational creature is fitted to cling to the Creator whose image it is, because this is the rational creature's sole good. As Saint David says: for me to cling to God is good. Obviously this clinging is not of the flesh but of the spirit, since the author of all natures inserted in this creature three things that allow it to share God's Eternity, participate in God's Wisdom and taste God's Sweetness. By these three I mean memory, understanding and love or will. Memory is capable of sharing God's Eternity, understanding God's Wisdom and love God's Sweetness. By these three the first man was fashioned in the image of the Trinity; his memory held fast to God without forgetfulness, his understanding recognized God without error and his love embraced God without a self-centred desire for anything else. And so this man was happy.[2]

Our first parent was endowed with free will and aided by God's grace. By a lasting love of God, and without it ever ending, he could have taken delight in the memory and knowledge of God and been everlastingly happy. But he could also divert his love to something less and so by withdrawing from God's love begin to grow cold and deliver himself up to misery. Now for a rational creature, just as there is no other happiness than to cling to God, so its misery is to withdraw from God. Although he was raised up and made to share in divine life, this man did not understand. He did not understand that those who by pride betray God stumble into foolishness and that anyone who by theft usurps the likeness of God is rightly garbed in the unlikeness of beasts.

By abusing free choice, then, the first man diverted his love from that changeless good and, blinded by his own self-centredness, he directed his love to what was inferior. Thus withdrawing from the true good and deviating toward what of itself was not good, where he anticipated gain he found loss. By perversely loving himself he lost both himself and God. Thus it very justly came about that someone who sought the likeness of God in defiance of God, the more he wanted to become similar to God out of curiosity, the more dissimilar he became through self-centredness. Therefore, the image of God became disfigured in us without becoming wholly destroyed. Consequently we have memory but it is subject to forgetfulness, understanding but it is open to error and love but it is prone to self-centredness.[3]

So God came after us in Christ and opened the way for us to return to God, restoring the divine likeness by charity.

Through Jesus Christ, the Mediator between God and us, the debt for which human nature was being held liable had at last been paid and the contract by which our ancient enemy with menacing pride held us bound had been destroyed. ... Then memory is restored by the words of Sacred Scripture, understanding by the mystery of faith and love by the daily increase of charity. The restoration of the image will be complete if no forgetfulness falsifies memory, if no error clouds our knowledge and no self-centredness claims our love.[4]

It is obvious, if I am not mistaken, that just as human pride, by departing from the supreme good not by footsteps but by the mind's attachment and becoming decrepit in itself, disfigured God's image in itself, so human humility, by approaching God by the spirit's attachment, restores the image of the Creator. Hence the Apostle says: Be renewed in the spirit of your mind and put on the new man who was created according to God. But how will this renewal come about except by the new precept of charity of which the Saviour says: I give you a new commandment. Then, if the mind puts on this charity perfectly, charity will straightway reform the other two, namely, memory and knowledge, which we said were equally disfigured. A summary of this one precept, then, is presented to us in a very salutary way; it contains the divesting of the old man, the renewal of his mind and the reforming of the divine image.[5]

Our struggle comes from the need to throw off the yoke of self-centredness.

Since only that power of the soul which is more usually called love is capable both of charity and of self-centredness this love is obviously divided against itself, as if by opposing appetites caused by the new infusion of charity and the remnants of a decrepit self-centredness. About this the Apostle says: I do not do what I will. And again: The flesh lusts against the spirit and the spirit against the flesh. These are so mutually opposed that you do not do the very things you will.[6]

To take Paul's words as our starting point, we say that the root of all evils is self-centredness just as, on the other hand, the root of all virtues is charity. As long as this poisonous root remains in the depths of the soul, even though some of the twigs on the surface may be pruned back, others will inevitably continue to sprout from the re-invigorated base until the very root from which these pernicious shoots spring up has been utterly torn out and nothing more remains. . . .

But if a mind is habituated to the very heavy yoke of self-centredness, its lax restfulness disguises itself as the sweetness of the Lord's yoke as long as there is no occasion for agitation. But as soon as some cause for indignation arises, the savage beast soon bursts from the recesses of the heart as if from a deeply hidden cavern. By the dreadful gnawing of the passions it tears and bloodies the poor soul, allowing it no time for peace or rest. So let this yoke rot in the presence of oil, that is to say, the yoke of self-centredness in the presence of charity. Then, all of a sudden, someone will experience how light, how easy, how joyful Christ's burden is; how, as someone has said, it catches one up to heaven and snatches one away from the earth.[7]

In and through charity all the virtues come to fullness.

All virtues exist together in charity and all exist together only in charity. Likewise in charity true tranquillity and true gentleness exist because charity is the Lord's yoke. If we bear this at the Lord's invitation we shall find rest for our souls because his yoke is easy and his burden light. In brief, charity is patient and kind, it is not jealous or conceited or boastful, is not ambitious and so on. For us, then, other virtues are like a carriage for someone weary, food for the traveller's journey, a lamp for those groping in darkness and weapons for those waging battle. But charity, which permits other virtues to be virtues, must exist in all the virtues. It is most particularly rest for the weary, an inn for the traveller, full light at journey's end and the perfect crown for the victor. For what is faith but a carriage to carry us to our fatherland? What is hope but food for the journey to support us in the miseries of this life? What are the four virtues – temperance, prudence, fortitude, and justice – but the weapons with which we wage battle? . . .

Temperance fights against lusts, prudence against errors, fortitude against adversities and justice against inequities. Yet in charity chastity is perfect and so there is no lust for temperance to fight. In charity knowledge is perfect and so there is no error for prudence to fight. In charity there is true happiness and so no adversity exists for fortitude to conquer. In charity everything is at peace and so there is no inequity against which justice must remain vigilant. Faith is not a virtue if it does not act through love nor hope a virtue if what is hoped for is not loved. If you look into this more closely, what is temperance but love that no sensual pleasure entices? What is prudence but love that no error seduces? What is fortitude but love bravely enduring adversity? What is justice but love righting with due moderation the iniquities of this life. Charity, then, begins in faith, is exercised in the other virtues and is perfected in itself.

This is charity, the consummation of all virtues, the agreeable refreshment of holy souls, the virtuous harmony of our conduct. This is the root from which all good works spring so that they may be good and in which all good works are perfected. The seventh day on which divine grace refreshes us, the month in which, after the deluge of temptations, the arc of the heart gently comes to rest. Temperance protects it, prudence keeps watch over it, fortitude fights for it and justice is its servant.[8]

The journey into the fullness of love, as Aelred develops it in his second book, requires that our perverse self-centredness with its threefold concupiscence – that of the flesh, of the eyes and a pride of life[9] – be turned about and healed through the threefold spiritual visitation. Here Aelred's doctrine of the spiritual journey presents the classical three stages in a refreshing way. The first visitation is a wake-up call to compunction and amendment. The second is one of consolation, nurturing us by 'draughts of divine sweetness',[10] purifying us in preparation for the third where we come to 'enjoy the tranquillity of the Sabbath'.[11] Aelred sees this as a reward.

> In the first state the soul is awakened, in the second it is purified and in the third it enjoys the tranquillity of the Sabbath. In the first state mercy is at work, in the second loving-kindness and in the third justice. For mercy seeks what is lost, loving-kindness reforms what is found and justice rewards what is already perfect. Mercy raises up one who is prostrate, loving-kindness aids one who combats and justice crowns the victor.[12]

He then inserts a dialogue with a novice (the dialogue form being one of his favourite literary fictions) to explore this teaching more concretely. He warns especially against judging by feelings and consolations rather than by one's action: 'The test of love is the demonstration of its activity.'[13]

Sometimes in tragedies or epic poetry, a character whose attractive handsomeness, admirable courage, and agreeable affections are extolled, is portrayed as persecuted or oppressed. If those hearing these things being sung or listening to them being recited are moved by some sort of affection even to the point of weeping, would it not be terribly absurd on this basis of worthless devotion to make some inference about the quality of those persons' love? Could it be claimed that such persons love one of the characters in the play for whose rescue they would not be willing to spend even a tiny part of what they possess, even if all these things really were taking place before his eyes? Likewise, if by God's inscrutable design we who are tepid and debauched and are touched with compunction because of some inward affection go back again to our empty, ludicrous and base ways after those sterile fears and momentary attachments. It is certainly foolish, and even more than that, it is insane, to come to this judgement about our love: that we are believed, because of these affections, to love God more than some who devote themselves so totally to God's service that they detest and have a deep horror of anything they know to be contrary to God's will and embrace with fervour any toil imposed on them in the Lord's name.[14]

It is in his third book of the *Mirror of Charity* that Aelred develops the fruit of love, using the biblical image of Sabbath. Just as there are in the Mosaic Law three Sabbaths – 'in the Law you have three times consecrated to the Sabbath rest: the seventh day, the seventh year and, after seven times seven, the fiftieth year'[15] – so there are three loves: love of self, neighbour and God.

Let love of self, then, be our first Sabbath; love of neighbour, the second, and love of God, the Sabbath of the
Sabbaths. As we said above, the spiritual Sabbath is rest
for the spirit, peace of heart and tranquillity of mind.
This Sabbath is sometimes experienced in love of one's
self, it is sometimes derived from the sweetness of brotherly or sisterly love and, beyond all doubt, it is brought
to perfection in the love of God. Surely a person should
be careful to love one's self in a suitable way, to love
one's neighbour as one's self and to love God more than
self and not to love either one's self or one's neighbour
except for God's sake.[16]

These three loves are engendered by one another, nourished by one another and fanned into flame by one another. Then they are all brought to perfection together.

What is more, it happens in a wondrous and ineffable
way that although all three of these loves are possessed
at the same time – for it cannot be otherwise – still all
three are not always sensed equally. At one moment
that rest and joy are sensed in the purity of one's own
conscience. At other time they are derived from the
sweetness of brotherly love. At another they are more
fully attained in the contemplation of God.[17]

Aelred interjects a rather extensive, practical and useful
study of 'attachment' and affection, concluding:

From all that has been said, then, let us briefly summarize what makes the whole force of love. First, if the
mind chooses something for its own enjoyment, then
reaches out to it by a kind of inward desire, and finally

does what will enable it to attain what it desires, this should without any doubt be called 'to love'. The more fervently and insistently someone then carries this through, the more does that one love. If we do this out of affection, we surely love more sweetly and therefore act with greater facility. If others do out of reason alone everything that we do solely by affection, they love less sweetly yet will not less promptly obtain what they desire.[18]

Then he goes on to speak of the 'enjoyment' that comes to us through love:

There is a temporal enjoyment by which we can enjoy one another in this life, as Paul enjoyed Philemnon. And there is an eternal enjoyment by which we shall enjoy one another in heaven, as the angels enjoy one another, in pure unity of mind. Moreover, since to enjoy means to experience something with gladness and delight, I think it evident that at present we by no means can enjoy everyone but only a few persons. It seems to me that we can turn to some people for testing, some for instruction, some for consolation and some for sustenance. We turn to our enemies for testing, our teachers for instruction, our elders for consolation and those supplying our needs for our sustenance. Only those whom we cherish with fond attachment, no matter which of these categories they may be in, do we turn to to sweeten our life and delight our spirit. These persons we can enjoy even at present, that is, we can find in them joy and delight. Charity can be shown to everyone by everyone in this life as far as the choice and interaction are concerned but as far as enjoyment is concerned, it can be shown to everyone only by a few or even by no one at all. There are few people, if there are any at all, who cherish every sort of human being not only with a rational but even with an affectionate love.

Finally, charity in both choice and action is shown toward God by many persons to whom the enjoyment of love is not granted in this life but is reserved for the ever-blessed vision of God after this life. There are some, too, who in the light of contemplation and the sweetness of compunction experience a beginning of this sweet enjoyment. But if we are looking toward future joys, these persons should not be said to enjoy God but rather to use God. God grants the ever-pleasant taste of divine sweetness to a good number of people more as a support for their weakness than as a fruit of their love.[19]

Spiritual Friendship

With this exposition on love Aelred sets the stage for his next major work – which proved to be the work of a lifetime – the *Spiritual Friendship*.

In this present life we are able to enjoy those whom we love not only by reason but also by affection. Among them, we especially take enjoyment in those who are linked to us more intimately and more closely by the pleasant bond of spiritual friendship. Lest someone think that this very holy sort of charity should seem reproachable, our Jesus himself, lowering himself to our condition in every way, suffering all things for us and being compassionate towards us, transformed it by manifesting his love. To one person, not to all, did he grant a resting place on his most sacred breast in token of his special love, so that the virginal head might be supported by the flowers of his virginal breast and the fragrant secrets of the heavenly bridal-chamber might instil the sweet scents of spiritual perfumes on his virginal affection more abundantly because more closely. So it is that even though all the disciples were cherished by the sweetness of supreme charity by the most blessed Master, still it was to this one that he accorded this name as a prerogative of yet more intimate attachment: that he would be called the disciple whom Jesus loved.[20]

In the final pages of the *Mirror* Aelred pens these beautiful lines about friendship:

Moreover, it is a wondrous consolation in this life to have someone with whom we can be united by an intimate attachment and the embrace of very holy love. To have someone in whom our spirit may rest, to whom we can pour out our soul, to whose gracious conversation we may flee for refuge amid sadness as to consoling songs or to the most generous bosom of whose friendship we may approach in safety amid the many troubles of this world. To whose most loving breast we may without hesitation confide all our inmost thoughts, as to ourselves, by whose spiritual kisses as by medicinal ointments we may sweat out of ourselves the weariness of agitating cares. Someone who will weep with us in anxiety, rejoice with us in prosperity, seek with us in doubts; someone we can let into the secret chamber of our mind by the bonds of love, so that even when absent in body that one is present in spirit. There, we alone may converse, we two alone, all the more sweetly because more secretly. Alone, we may speak we two alone and once the noise of the world is hushed, in the sleep of peace, we alone may repose we two alone in the embrace of charity, the kiss of unity, with the sweetness of the Holy Spirit flowing between us. Still more, we may be so united we two and approach each other so closely and so mingle our spirits that the two become one.[21]

Aelred's dialogue on spiritual friendship which he presents as the fruit of several encounters which took place over the course of many years is his best-known contribution to Christian spirituality. To be properly understood it has to be seen as flowing out of the whole context presented in the *Mirror of Charity*.

When Aelred entered Rievaulx he brought in with him (as does every monk, from Bernard of Clairvaux to Thomas Merton) his individuality and his life's experiences. This is evident in Aelred's writing which touch upon the history and nobility of his times, the saints of its shrines and his sister's vocation as well as those things that deeply touched his own personal life. Aelred's study in his youth of the *De amicitia* (*On Friendship*) of Marcus Tullius Cicero which was an important part of every classical education, many years later remains the humanist fabric into which he weaves the fullness of the gospel's call to friendship as taught and exemplified by Christ and lived in its fullness in the most blessed Trinity.

The teaching of this dialogue is important as the elaboration and fulfilment of Aelred's basic teaching in the *Mirror of Charity*, where already he had begun to set forth his theological and pastoral understanding of this way of Christian holiness. While friendship among men, which would blossom in an almost mythological chivalry, is one of the great literary themes of the Middle Ages, finding its basis in Sacred Scripture as well as classical texts, Aelred's contribution is significant because it is so really personal and so profoundly God-centred without losing any of its rich humanism. Unlike his great Christian master, Augustine of Hippo, for Aelred, speaking from his own life's experience, the flow from physical love filled with sentiment and emotion to something more platonic and on ultimately to divine love was a continuous unbroken movement. For Aelred it is an ideal worth striving for, worth the high price it costs, for it is a way to true holiness and complete fulfilment.

First Aelred with his interlocutor explores the nature of friendship.

Ivo: In the first place, I think we should discuss the nature of friendship so as not to appear to be painting in emptiness, as we would, indeed, if we were unaware of the precise identity of that about which an ordered discussion on our part should proceed.

Aelred: But surely you are satisfied, as a starting point, with what Tullius [Cicero] says, are you not? 'Friendship is mutual harmony in affairs human and divine coupled with benevolence and charity.'

Ivo: If that definition satisfies you, I agree that it satisfies me.

Aelred: In that case, those who have the same opinion,

the same will, in matters human and divine, along with mutual benevolence and charity, have, we shall admit, reached the perfection of friendship.

Ivo: Why not? But still, I do not see what the pagan Cicero meant by the word 'charity' and 'benevolence'.

Aelred: Perhaps for him the word 'charity' expresses an affection of the heart and the word 'benevolence', carrying it out in deed. For mutual harmony itself in matters human and divine ought to be dear to the hearts of both, that is, attractive and precious and the carrying out of these works in actual practice ought to be both benevolent and pleasant. ... You can, however, get some idea of the nature of friendship from the definition, even though it should seem somewhat imperfect.

Ivo: Please, will I annoy you if I say that this definition does not satisfy me unless you unravel for me the meaning of the word itself?

Aelred: I should be glad to comply with your wishes if only you will pardon my lack of knowledge and not force me to teach what I do not know. Now I think the word *amicus* [friend] comes from the word *amor* [love], and *amicitia* [friendship] from *amicus*. For love is a certain 'affection' of the rational soul whereby it seeks and eagerly strives after some object to possess it and enjoy it. Having attained its object through love it enjoys it with a certain interior sweetness, embraces it and preserves it.[22]

It is important to realize that there is a difference between charity and friendship 'for divine authority approves that more are to be received into the bosom of charity than into the embrace of friendship. For we are compelled by the law of charity to receive in the embrace of love not only our friends but also our enemies. But only those do we call friends to whom we can fearlessly entrust our heart and all its secrets; those, too, who, in turn, are bound to us by the same law of faith and security.'[23]

Aelred sees three kinds of friendship:

Let one kind of friendship be called carnal, another worldly and another spiritual. The carnal springs from mutual harmony in vice; the worldly is enkindled by the hope of gain; and the spiritual is cemented by similarity of life, morals and pursuits among the just. The real beginning, carnal friendship, proceeds from an affection which like a harlot directs its step after every passer-by, following its own lustful ears and eyes in every direction.[24]

Worldly friendship, which is born of a desire for temporal advantage or possessions, is always full of deceit and intrigue; it contains nothing certain, nothing constant, nothing secure; for, to be sure, it ever changes with fortune and follows the purse. Hence it is written: 'He is a fair-weather friend and he will not abide in the day of your trouble.' Take away his hope of profit and immediately he will cease to be a friend. This type of friendship the following lines very aptly deride:

A friend, not of the man, but of his purse is he,
Held fast by fortune fair, by evil made to flee.[25]

Spiritual friendship, which we call true, should be desired, not for consideration of any worldly advantage or for any extrinsic cause but from the dignity of its own nature and the feelings of the human heart so that its fruition and reward is nothing other than itself.[26]

Echoing William's 'unity of spirit' and the opening theme of Bernard's *Sermons on the Song of Songs*, Aelred sees friendship as a stage towards friendship with God.

In friendship there is nothing dishonourable, nothing deceptive, nothing feigned. Whatever there is, is holy, voluntary, and true. . . . In friendship are joined honour and charm, truth and joy, sweetness and good-will, affection and action. And all these take their beginning from Christ, advance through Christ and are perfected in Christ. Therefore, not too steep or unnatural does the ascent appear from Christ, as the inspiration of the love by which we love our friend, to Christ giving himself to us as our Friend for us to love, so that charm may follow upon charm, sweetness upon sweetness and affection upon affection. And thus, friend cleaving to friend in the spirit of Christ is made with Christ but one heart and one soul. And so mounting aloft through degrees of love to friendship with Christ, we are made one spirit with him in one kiss. Aspiring to this kiss the saintly one cries out: 'Let him kiss me with the kiss of his mouth.'[27]

Ivo: What does this all add up to? Shall I say of friendship what John, the friend of Jesus, says of charity: 'God is friendship'?

Aelred: That would be unusual, to be sure, nor does it have the sanction of the Scriptures. But still what is true of charity, I surely do not hesitate to grant to friendship, since the one who abides in friendship, abides in God, and God in that person.[28]

This is that extraordinary and great happiness which we await, with God acting and diffusing, between God and God's creatures whom God has uplifted, among the very degrees and orders which God has distinguished among the individual souls whom God has chosen. So much friendship and charity, that thus each one of us loves another as we do ourselves. By this means, just as each one of us rejoices in our own, so do we rejoice in the good fortune of another and thus the happiness of each one individually is the happiness of all and the universality of all happiness is the possession of each individual. There one finds no hiding of thoughts, no dissembling of affection. This is true and eternal friendship that begins in this life and is perfected in the next, which here belongs to the few where few are good but there belongs to all where all are good.[29]

In good Cistercian fashion Aelred brings this to Christ:

How delightful friends find it to converse with one another, mutually to reveal their interests, to examine all things together and to agree on all of them! Added to this there is prayer for one another, which, coming from a friend, is the more efficacious in proportion as it is more lovingly sent to God, with tears which either fear excites or affection awakens or sorrow evokes. And thus a friend praying to Christ on behalf of his friend and for his friend's sake desiring to be heard by Christ, directs his attention with love and longing to Christ. Then it sometimes happens that quickly and imperceptibly the one love passes over into the other and coming, as it were, into close contact with the sweetness of

Christ himself, the friend begins to taste his sweetness and to experience his charm. Thus ascending from that holy love with which he embraces a friend to that with which he embraces Christ, he will joyfully partake in abundance of the spiritual fruit of friendship, awaiting the fullness of all things in the life to come.[30]

We must be clear as to what is the foundation of this friendship and how we might grow in it.

In the first place, one ought to lay a solid foundation for spiritual love itself and in this foundation its principles ought to be set down, so that those who are mounting straight up to its higher levels may not neglect or go beyond its foundation but observe the greatest caution. That foundation is the love of God to which all things that either love or affection suggests, all that secretly any spirit or openly any friend recommends must be referred. Moreover, one ought to observe carefully that whatever is built thereon conforms to the foundation. Have no doubt that whatever is seen as going beyond this foundation ought to be brought back into conformity with its plan and set right according to its nature.[31]

Four elements in particular seem to pertain to friendship: namely, love and affection, security and happiness. Love implies the rendering of services with benevolence; affection, an inward pleasure that manifests itself exteriorly; security, a revelation of all councils and confidences without fear and suspicion; happiness, a pleasing and friendly sharing of all events which occur, whether joyful or sad, of all thoughts, whether harmful or useful, of everything taught or learned.[32]

Aelred speaks at length about careful selection of friends, indicating that certain defects of character preclude friendship:

Speaking of selection, we excluded the quarrelsome, the irascible, the fickle, the suspicious and the loquacious; and yet not all, but only those who are unable or unwilling to regulate or restrain these passions. For many are affected by these disturbances in such a manner that their perfection is not only in no way injured, but their virtue is even more laudably increased by the restraint of these passions. For men, who, as though unbridled, are carried away headlong under the impulse of these passions, inevitably slip and fall into those vices by which friendship, as Scripture testifies, is wounded and dissolved: namely, insults, reproaches, the betrayal of secrets, pride and the stroke of treachery.[33]

He moves on towards his consideration of spiritual friendship giving this beautiful testimony:

The day before yesterday, as I was walking the round of the cloister of the monastery, the brethren were sitting around forming, as it were, a most loving crown. In the midst, as it were, of the delights of paradise with the leaves, flowers and fruits of each single tree, I marvelled. In that multitude of brethren I found no one whom I did not love and no one by whom, I felt sure, I was not loved. I was filled with such joy that it surpassed all the delights of this world. I felt, indeed, my spirit transfused into all and the affection of all to have passed into me, so that I could say with the Prophet: 'Behold, how good and how pleasant it is for brethren to dwell together in unity.'[34]

Then he concretizes his teaching by candidly sharing some of his own experiences. This sharing not only teaches us a good deal about friendship as it was experienced in Cistercian life but it also tells us much about Aelred and life at Rievaulx.

> I recall now two friends, who, although they have passed from this present life, nevertheless live to me and always will so live. The first of these I gained as my friend when I was still young, in the beginning of my conversion, because of a certain resemblance between us in character and similarity of interests. The other I chose when he was still a boy and after I had tested him repeatedly in various ways, when at length age was silvering my hair, I admitted him into my most intimate friendship. Indeed, I chose the former as my companion, as the one who shared in the delights of the cloister and the spiritual joys which I was just beginning to taste, when I, too, was not as yet burdened with any pastoral duty or concerned with temporal affairs. I demanded nothing and I bestowed nothing but affection and the loving judgement of affection according as charity dictated. The latter I claimed when he was still young to be a sharer in my anxieties and a co-worker in these labours of mine.
> Looking back, as far as my memory permits, upon each of these friendships, I see that the first rested for

the most part on affection and the second on reason, although affection was not lacking in the latter nor reason in the former. In fine, my first friend, taken from me in the very beginnings of our friendship, I was able to choose, as I have said, but not to test. The other devoted to me from boyhood even to middle age and loved by me, mounted with me through all the stages of friendship, as far as human imperfection permitted. And indeed, it was my admiration for his virtues that first directed my affection toward him. It was I who long ago brought him from the south to this northern solitude and first introduced him to regular discipline. From that time he learned to conquer his own flesh and to endure labour and hunger. To very many he was an example, to many a source of admiration and to myself a source of honour and delight.

Already at that time I thought that he should be nurtured in the beginnings of friendship, seeing that he was a burden to no one but pleasing to all. He came and went, hastening at the command of his superiors, humble, gentle, reserved, sparing of speech, a stranger to indignation and unacquainted with murmuring, rancour and detraction. He walked as one deaf, hearing not, and as one dumb not opening his mouth. 'He became as a beast of burden',[35] submissive to the reins of obedience, bearing untiringly the yoke of regular discipline in mind and body. Once when he was still young he was in the infirmary and he was rebuked by my holy father and predecessor for yielding so early in life to rest and inactivity. The boy was so ashamed at this that he immediately left the infirmary and subjected himself with such zeal to corporal labour that for many years he would not allow himself any relaxation from his accustomed rigour, even when he was afflicted with serious illness. All this in a most wondrous way had bound him to me by the most intimate bonds and had so brought him into my affection that from an inferior I made him my companion, from a companion a friend, from a friend my most cherished of friends.

When I saw that he had advanced far in the life of virtue and grace I consulted the brethren and imposed upon him the burden of the sub-prior's office. This went against his will, to be sure, but because he had vowed himself to obedience, he modestly accepted. Yet he pleaded with me in secret to be relieved of it, alleging as excuse his age, his lack of knowledge and finally the friendship which we had but lately formed. He feared that this might prove to be an occasion for him either to love the less or to be loved the less. But, availing nothing by these entreaties, then he began to reveal quite freely but at the same time humbly and modestly what he feared for each of us and what in me pleased him but little. He hoped thereby, as he afterwards confessed, that I would be offended by this presumption and would the more easily be inclined to grant his request. But his freedom of speech and spirit only led our friendship to its culmination, for my desire for his friendship was lessened not a whit.

Perceiving then that his words had pleased me and that I answered humbly to each accusation and had satisfied him in all these matters and that he himself had not only caused no offence but rather had benefited more, he began to manifest his love for me even more ardently than theretofore, to relax the reins of his affection and to reveal himself wholly to me. In this way we tested one another, I making proof of his freedom of utterance and he of my patience. And I, too, repaid my friend in kind in his turn. At an opportune moment thinking that I should harshly reprove him, I did not spare him any reproaches and I found him patient with my frankness and grateful. Then I began to reveal to him the secrets of my innermost thoughts and I found him faithful. In this way love increased between us, affection glowed warmer and charity was strengthened until we attained that point where we had but one mind and one soul to will and to not will alike. Our love was devoid of fear and knew no offence. It shunned suspicion and abhorred flattery. There was no pretence between us, no simulation, no dishonourable words, no unbecoming harshness, no evasion, no concealment. Everything was open and above board for I deemed my heart his and his mine. And he felt in like manner towards me.

And so we progressed in friendship without any deviation. Neither's correction evoked the indignation of the other, neither's yielding produced blame. So, proving himself a friend in every respect, he provided as much as was in his power for my peace and my rest. He exposed himself to dangers and he forestalled scandals in their very inception. Occasionally I wanted to provide for his ailments with some creature comforts but he opposed it, saying that we should be on our guard against having our love measured according to the consolations of the flesh and of having the gift ascribed to my carnal affection rather than to his need with the resultant effect that my authority might be diminished. He was as it were, my hand, my eye, the staff of my old age. He was the refuge of my spirit, the sweet solace of my grief. His loving heart received me when I was fatigued by labours. His counsel refreshed me when I was plunged into sadness and sorrow. He brought calmness to my soul when I was distressed, he soothed me when I was angry. Whenever anything unpleasant occurred, I turned to him so that, shoulder to shoulder, I was able to bear more easily what I could not bear alone.

What more is there, then, that I can say? Was it not a foretaste of blessedness thus to love and to be loved, thus to help and to be helped? And in this way from the sweetness of fraternal charity to wing one's flight aloft to the sublime splendour of divine love? And by the ladder of charity now to mount to the embrace of Christ himself and then again to descend to find pleasant rest in a neighbour's love?[36]

This picture is complemented by the long and beautiful eulogy for his friend and confrere, Simon, which Aelred placed at the end of the first book of the *Mirror of Charity*. Friendship played a large and important part in the lives of Aelred, William and Bernard as they grew and became masters in the 'school of love' that is Citeaux.

4

EVERYDAY HOLINESS
Guerric of Igny

Bernard of Clairvaux must have had greater power to attract than just about any person who ever lived. Without exaggeration, every time he went out of his monastery he returned with some fifty or a hundred men in his train. In 1123 one of those who followed him home was Guerric, a scholar and probably a master at the school of Tournai. For the next fifteen years Guerric sat quietly at the feet of Bernard, drinking in the wisdom of the school of love. Then in 1138 he was elected abbot of one of Clairvaux's daughter houses, Igny. As abbot he was called upon to preach to the whole community on sixteen occasions in the course of the year. Towards the end of his life, Guerric decided to make a collection of his sermons, gathering five from each of the days on which he had preached. Unfortunately he died before he was able to complete this task so we have only fifty-three sermons in the collection. We are fortunate, though, in the fact that these sermons have been little edited for publication so they give us one of the closest examples we have of the talks that a Cistercian Father would have given to his community. Guerric is very down to earth, simple, and practical, but he never loses sight of the sublime heights to which we are called.

The Cistercian Way to Holiness

Like several other Cistercian Fathers Guerric took the
Feast of All Saints, on which the eight Beatitudes are pro-
claimed in the Gospel reading of the day, as an opportunity to outline the Cistercian way to holiness. His outline
is far simpler than that of Aelred, who amplified his presentation by bringing in not only the seven gifts of the
Spirit recounted in Isaiah and the six days of creation from
Genesis, but the evening and morning of each day. Nor is
Guerric's presentation as developed as Bernard's. However, we possess only one of Guerric's All Saints sermons,
and perhaps we would have seen the way developed
much more in the other sermons he intended to add to the
collection.

Be that as it may, Guerric traces out this path for us:

In this arrangement of the virtues in a series of eight
steps there can clearly be seen a certain stairway for the
heart and a progression in merits. We are led step by step
from the lowest states of evangelical perfection to the
very highest until we enter the temple on Sion and behold the God of gods. It was in reference to this temple
that the Prophet speaks: 'And the ascent to it was by
eight steps.'[1]

The first virtue in this ascent, proper to beginners,
is renunciation of the world, which makes us poor in
spirit. The second is meekness, which enables us to sub-
mit ourselves in obedience and to accustom ourselves to
such submission. Next comes mourning to make us
weep for our sins and to beg God for virtue. It is here
that we first taste justice, and so learn to hunger and

thirst more keenly after justice in ourselves as well as in others and we begin to be roused to zeal against sinful men. Then, lest this zeal should grow immoderate and lead to vice, mercy follows to temper it. When we have learned to become merciful and just by diligent practice of these virtues we will then perhaps be fit to enter upon the way of contemplation and to give ourselves to the task of obtaining that purity of heart which will enable us to see God. Tested and proved in this way in both the active and the contemplative life, we who bear the name and office of a child of God through our having become the parent and servant of others will then and only then be worthy to be a peacemaker between them and God. Thus we will fulfil the office of mediator and advocate and be worthy to make peace within the community and even between the community and those who are outside. For thus it is written in praise of our holy Fathers: 'They were men bringing peace in their houses.'[2] If we are faithful and constant in this office, we will often attain that virtue and merit which belongs to the martyr, who suffers persecution for justice's sake and this even on occasion at the hands of those for whom we are fighting. . . .[3]

He goes on to add in true Benedictine spirit:

What I have said is not new to you, my brethren, but I still want to impress upon you that truly blessed poverty of spirit is to be found more in humility of heart than in a mere privation of everyday possessions, and it consists more in the renunciation of pride than in a mere contempt for property. Sometimes it may be useful to own things, but it is never anything but mortally dangerous to hold on to pride. The devil owns nothing in this world nor does he desire to own anything; it is pride and pride alone that damns him.

Humility is the standard of Christ, pride is that of Antichrist, or rather pride is the standard of his leader the devil, who has command over all the children of pride; pride was his sin from the very beginning.[4]

The Exercises of Wisdom

With Cistercian practicality Guerric notes that the wisdom of this way can not be retained nor followed except by concrete practices: 'Now to achieve this wisdom of continuing in wisdom, it is most important, I think, not readily to allow restlessness or any kind of provocation to keep us away from any of the exercises of wisdom: the divine office, personal prayer, *lectio divina*, our daily labour or the practice of quietness.'[5] With certain insight, Guerric reminds us that when we are taking part in the office or praying we should be conscious of a twofold listening. First of all, we are being listened to:

Friends, that is, angels, are listening to us as we pray or sing psalms. . . . In this let us consider with what discipline of heart and body we ought to sing psalms or pray in the sight of the angels lest they be sent away empty and send us away empty, they who had come to carry our prayers up and bring back gifts. . . . The Bridegroom himself, who stands at the door and knocks, if no worthy devotion answers him from within and opens the door, will go away complaining. . . .'[6]

But we, too, are to be listeners when we pray:

> For it is the mark of a friend to listen devotedly to the Bridegroom's voice, as John says: the Bridegroom's friend is he who stands by, not wandering in mind or prostrated by sleep, and listens, rejoices too, rejoices at hearing the Bridegroom's voice which he recognizes even in his servants. Let us then also, whether the Bridegroom's voice sounds through the mouth of one speaking or reading or singing, prove ourselves to be friends by so standing and listening that it may give joy and gladness to our hearing and we may not only receive the word with joy but also bear fruit in patience.[7]

This listening carries over into the basic practice of *lectio divina*:

> Search the Scriptures then. For you are not mistaken in thinking that you find life in them, you who seek nothing else in them but Christ, to whom the Scriptures bear witness. Blessed indeed are they who search his testimonies, seek them out with all their heart. 'Your testimonies are wonderful, Lord, therefore my soul has searched them.'[8] There is need for searching not only in order to draw out the mystical sense but also to taste the moral sense. Therefore you who walk about in the gardens of the Scriptures do not pass by heedlessly and idly but searching each and every word like busy bees gathering honey from flowers, reap the Spirit from the words. 'For my Spirit,' says Jesus, 'is sweeter than honey and my inheritance surpasses the honeycomb.'[9]

A listening spirit, a sense of the Divine Presence, is not to be left behind when we leave the exercises we most readily connect with prayer. It is for this reason that Guerric, following St Paul, not only encourages work but links it with quietness:

> In order then, my brethren, that he who loves quiet and bestows it may rest in you, make a point, as the Apostle advises, of being quiet. How will this come about? 'I tell you,' he says, 'to attend to your own business and to work with your hands.'[10] Work is a load by which, as ships are given weight so hearts are given quiet and gravity, and in it the outward man finds a firm foundation and a settled condition.[11]

> Let us all then together so make a point of being quiet that in our quiet we may always be occupied with meditation on eternal quiet and for desire of it be found ready for every work.[12]

And he concludes in truest Cistercian fashion: 'May the blessed Mother of God obtain this for us by her prayers from him who rested in the tabernacle of her body and her heart.'[13]

5

THE MASTER OF THE SCHOOL
Bernard of Clairvaux

Finally we come to the master of the school of love, the pious son (one of five) of Tescelin, the Lord of Fontaines-les-Dijon, and his wife, Aleth of Montbard. In the end, it was the seemingly frail and studious son who stayed at home who conquered his brothers who had gone off to battle, leading them, along with his father, to the gates of Citeaux.

Abbot Stephen could hardly ignore such leadership qualities. Shortly after his profession Bernard was sent off at the head of a band of twelve to change the Valley of Bitterness into a valley of light, Clairvaux.

Let Me Sing of a Maiden

Knowing the Cistercian charism as we do, we are not surprised to discover that during those first years of his abbatial service, when he was still hardly known and relatively free, Bernard devoted himself to singing the praises of the Lady of Citeaux, the holy Virgin Mary. His four homilies commenting on the Gospel account of the Annunciation are exquisitely beautiful. Here we find Bernard's most beautiful *Respice Stellam*, Look at the Star.

'The Virgin's name was Mary.' Let us now say a few words about this name, which means 'star of the sea' and is so becoming the Virgin Mother. Surely she is very fittingly likened to a star. . . . O you, whoever you are, who feel in the tidal wave of this world you are nearer to being tossed about among the squalls and gales than treading on dry land, if you do not want to founder in the tempest, do not avert your eyes from the brightness of the Star. When the wind of temptation blows up within you, when you strike upon the rock of tribulation, gaze up at the Star, call out to Mary. Whether you are being tossed about by the waves of pride or ambition or slander or jealousy, gaze up at this Star, call out to Mary. When rage or greed or fleshly desires are battering the skiff of your soul, gaze up at Mary. When the immensity of your sins weighs you down and you are bewildered by the loathesomeness of your conscience, when the terrifying thought of judgement appalls you and you begin to founder in the gulf of sadness and despair, think of Mary. In dangers, in hardships, in every doubt, think of Mary, call out to Mary. Keep her in your mouth, keep her in your heart. Follow the example of her life and you obtain the favour of her prayer. Following her you will never go astray. Asking her help, you will never despair. Keeping her in your thoughts, you will never wander away. With your hand in hers, you will never stumble. With her protecting you, you will not be afraid. With her leading you, you will never tire. Her kindness will see you through to the end. Then you will know from your own experience how true it is that 'the Virgin's name was Mary'.[1]

As beautiful as this is, it is a portion of a later sermon that stands out in one's memory as expressing the fullness of Mary's role, the analogy of the aqueduct in Bernard's Sermon for the Nativity of the Virgin. Divine grace flows to us from the Father's heart through the holy Virgin.

Now what is the fountain of life if it be not Christ the Lord? This stream from the heavenly source descends to us through an aqueduct. The aqueduct does not show all the fullness of the fountain but it moistens our dry and withered hearts with some few drops of grace, giving more to one, less to another. The aqueduct is always full, so that all may receive of its fullness.

You must have already guessed, dear Brothers and Sisters, to whom I allude under the image of an aqueduct, which receiving the fullness of the Fountain from the Father's heart has passed it on to us, at least in so far as we can contain it. You know it was she to whom it was said, 'Hail, full of grace.'[2]

But how did this Aqueduct of ours attain to the loftiness of the Fountain? How indeed, except by the ardour of her desires, by the fervour of her devotion, by the purity of her prayer? How did she reach up even to the inaccessible Majesty but by knocking, by asking, by seeking? And she found what she was seeking, since it was said to her: 'You have found favour with God.'[3]

First Comes Humility

Central to Benedictine spirituality and therefore to Cistercian spirituality is the virtue of humility. Benedict devotes a whole long chapter to this virtue alone, tracing through twelve steps our whole journey to transforming union. While Cistercian abbots preached to the whole community on only sixteen occasions in the course of the year, the choir monks would gather in chapter each morning after chanting the Office of Prime to hear a chapter of Benedict's Rule. This would give the abbot an opportunity to comment on it. Bernard's comments were rich, deep, full of wisdom and humour. It is not surprising then that when Godfrey, his prior, was being sent forth to start a new monastery, he asked Bernard for his commentary on this central chapter of the Rule. Bernard spoke more on the mirror of the steps of humility, the steps of pride – claiming greater familiarity with them – especially warning his monks against the first step of pride, curiosity, which could lead to a swift descent to the depths.

The first step of pride is curiosity. How does it show itself? Now you begin to notice that wherever you are, standing, walking or sitting, your eyes are wondering, your glance darts right and left, your ears are cocked. Some change has taken place in you, every movement shows it. 'The perverse person winks the eye, nudges the foot, points the finger.'[4] These symptoms show your soul has caught some disease. You used to watch over your own conduct, now all your watchfulness is for others. 'They do not know themselves so they must go forth to pasture their goats.'[5] Goats are a symbol of sin and I am applying the word to their eyes and ears. They are the windows through which death creeps into the soul, as death came into the world by sin. These are the flocks the curious tend while they let their soul starve.

My Friend, if you gave yourself the attention you

ought, I do not think you would have much time to look after others. Listen, Busybody, to Solomon. Listen to the words of the Wise Man for a fool: 'Guard your heart with all care.'[6] Your senses have quite enough to do to guard the source of life. You wander away from yourself? Whom have you left in charge? Your eyes sweep the heavens. How do you dare, you who have sinned against heaven? Look over the earth, that you might know yourself. It speaks to you of yourself because, 'dust you are and unto dust you shall return'.[7]

Are the eyes never to be raised at all?

Yes, but only for two reasons: to look for help or to help others. David raised his eyes to the mountains to see if help would come to him. Our Lord looked out over the crowd to see if they needed his help. One raised his eyes in misery, the other in mercy – two excellent reasons. If when time, place and circumstances call for it, you raise your eyes for your own need or your sister's or brother's, I certainly will not blame you. I will think all the better of you. Misery is a good excuse. Mercy is a very commendable reason.[8]

Bernard does not content himself to explore the virtue of humility. He makes clear what is the purpose of the ladder of humility. And here in summary he traces out the Cistercian way to holiness.

If you want to know the full truth about yourself you will have to get rid of the beam of pride which blocks out the light from your eye and then set up in your heart the ladder of humility so that you can search into yourself. When you have climbed its twelve steps you will then stand on the first step of truth. When you have seen the truth about yourself, or better, when you have seen yourself in the truth, you will be able to say: 'I believed, therefore I have spoken but I have been exceedingly humbled.'[9] . . . I came to know Christ, to imitate his humility. I saw the truth and exalted it in me by my confession, but 'I myself was humbled exceedingly.' In my own eyes, I fell very low. The Psalmist has been humbled and now stands on the first step of truth.

When in the light of Truth people know themselves . . . they fly from justice to mercy, by the road Truth shows them: 'Blessed are the merciful for they shall obtain mercy.'[10] They look beyond their own needs to the needs of their neighbours and from the things they themselves have suffered they learn compassion: they have come to the second degree of truth.

If they persevere in these things: sorrow of repentance, desire for justice and works of mercy, they will cleanse their hearts from the three impediments of ignorance, weakness and jealousy and will come through contemplation to the third degree of truth.

These are the three steps of truth. We climb to the first by the toil of humility, to the second by deep feelings of compassion and to the third by the ecstacy of contemplation. On the first step we experience the severity of truth, on the second its tenderness, on the third its purity. Reason brings us to the first as we judge ourselves; compassion brings us to the second when we have mercy on others; on the third the purity of truth sweeps us up to the sight of things invisible.[11]

Grace, Freedom and Contemplation

Bernard not only sees the spiritual journey as a journey into the knowledge and experience of Truth but also a journey into freedom. In his most theological treatise, *On Grace and Free Choice*, he develops this at length, again having recourse to a tripartite distinction.

> There are three kinds of freedom, as they occur to us: freedom from sin, freedom from sorrow and freedom from necessity. The last belongs to our natural condition, the first we are restored to by grace and the second is reserved for us in our homeland.
>
> The first freedom might be termed freedom of nature; the second, of grace; and the third, of life or glory. At first we were created with free will and voluntary freedom, a creature noble in God's eyes. Secondly, we are re-formed in innocence, a new creature in Christ. And thirdly, we are raised up to glory, a perfect creation in the Spirit. The first freedom is thus a title of considerable honour; the second, of even greater power; and the last, of total happiness. By the first, we have the advantage over other living things; by the second, over the flesh; by the third, we overcome death itself.[12]
>
> But what of those who at times, being caught up in the Spirit through the ecstasy of contemplation, become capable of savouring something of the sweetness of heavenly bliss? Do these attain to freedom from sorrow as often as this happens to them? Yes, indeed. Even in this present life those who with Mary have chosen the better part – which shall not be taken away from them –

enjoy freedom of pleasure; rarely, however, and fleetingly. This is undeniable. For those who possess now
that which shall never be taken away, plainly experience
what is to come. In a word, happiness. And since happiness and sorrow are incompatible, as often as these
participate through the Spirit in the former they cease
to feel the latter. Hence, on this earth, contemplatives
alone can in some way enjoy freedom of pleasure,
though only in part, in a sufficiently modest part, and
on very rare occasions.[13]

Let Him Kiss Me

Having heard Bernard trace out the spiritual journey
through three stages of truth and through the acquisition
of the three freedoms, we are not surprised, when we
come to his masterly work, his *Sermons on the Song of
Songs*, to find him again and again having recourse to a
threesome. First he assigns three books of Scripture to the
three stages: the Book of Ecclesiastes which first enlightens
the mind, the Book of Proverbs which teaches true discipline, and finally the Song of Songs which leads us in the
way of union. Following the lead of the opening words of
this last book, Bernard then speaks of the three kisses: the
kiss of the feet of the Lord in conversion and repentance,
knowing God's mercy and justice; the kiss of the hands in
gratitude and collaboration, celebrating God's liberality
and fortitude; 'and finally, when we shall have obtained
these favours through many prayers and tears, we humbly
dare to raise our eyes to his mouth, so divinely beautiful,
not merely to gaze upon it, but – I say with fear and trembling – to receive his kiss'.[14] Continuing to develop these,

in Sermon 10 Bernard recapitulates his doctrine speaking of three ointments: that of contrition poured out on the feet of the Lord, devotion poured out on his head, and piety poured out on his whole body, the Church.

Thus we might recapitulate the three stages that are traced out by St Bernard in these first twelve sermons on the Song of Songs: The first stage, that of conversion, which is guided by the wisdom of the Book of Ecclesiastes, is imaged in the kiss of the feet and the pungent odour of the ointment of contrition. It responds to the divine justice and mercy with fear and repentance and a lively hope. The second stage, that of the active life (in the earlier sense of the term, the development of the virtues), which is guided by the wisdom of the Book of Proverbs, is imaged in the kiss of the hands and the ointment of devotion. It experiences the divine liberality and strength through reflecting upon God's long-suffering and benignity, above all in the redemptive goodness of Jesus Christ. It responds with perseverance in good works, humble gratitude and an intense longing for an ever-deeper union, an ever-fuller union with such goodness. Finally, the third stage, that of the contemplative life, which is illuminated by the wisdom of the Song of Songs, is imaged by the kiss of the mouth and the ointment of pity and compassion. It delights in the experience of the indwelling Spirit with her infusions of understanding and love which overflow to all about us in encouragement, compassion and effective mercy, stretching out in concern to the whole Body of Christ.

6

LET'S BE PRACTICAL –
VERY PRACTICAL

Fundamental to the Cistercian reform and the ongoing
living of the Cistercian way is a wholehearted devotion to
the Rule we profess as a way to live the gospel call to the
full. It is only by a well-regulated life that we can obtain
the freedom – the freedom of spirit as well as the time and
space – to enter fully into that intimate relationship with
God that we are to have in Christ. *Lectio* grounds our life,
for faith comes through hearing, hearing the Word of
God. In contemplation we most fully realize here on the
journey that towards which we live. The time for these
two basic features is sacred and given high priority in our
lives. But they are in fact just expressions of a whole,
a relationship that finds place in all that we do and say
and are. If these basic elements of Cistercian spirituality
are to be integrated into the lives of men and women who
are still called to pursue active lives in the world, then
some simple, practical, concrete instruction in regard
to them might be most useful. That is what is offered
here.

Lectio divina

The Lord is truly present in his Word. Holy Spirit who
guided the writers and editors of these sacred texts abides
in them and in us, to enable us to hear. We do well to

enthrone, in some way, the sacred text in our homes so that we can be conscious of this presence.

When our time for *lectio* is at hand, we want to approach the text with reverence, coming into the divine presence. And we want to call upon Holy Spirit to help us, as Jesus promised she would, to hear and understand.

Then we want not to read, but to listen, letting the Lord speak to us through his holy Word. It is well to set a certain amount of time for this meeting with the Lord, a minimal time that we will be faithful to each day, knowing we can always extend it if we wish and are able. We set a time, rather than a quantity, for the Lord might speak to us in the first word or sentence and we will want to stay there.

At the end of our time, we thank the Lord. How good God is to come to us in his Word and speak to us, unworthy though we are. And we take some word, sentence or phrase with us. Sometimes such a word is given to us, striking us deeply as we listen. At other times we have to choose one.

Towards Continual Prayer

This is the way we move towards fulfilling the Lord's command to pray without ceasing, to pray continually. We carry with us a word or phrase from our *lectio*. We let it repeat itself in our mind and even on our lips. Through it we let the Lord speak to us as we move along through the day. (Remember Guerric's word on quietness and work.) And we respond as is appropriate. Through it the Lord will sometimes throw new light on what we are experiencing, share his insight with us. Sometimes it will

prove to be just the word needed by someone else, someone we encounter that day.

This is what the early Church understood by *meditatio*,
meditation. Letting a received word repeat itself in the
mind and on the lips until it formed the heart and called
forth a response: *oratio*, prayer.

Contemplative Prayer

'Be still and know that I am God.'[1] Then there is the time
to let everything else go and simply rest in God, in God's
love. When one has extended periods for *lectio*, as do
monks and nuns, such times come as it were naturally. But
when we have to respond to all the demands of a very
active life, then it is necessary to set aside times to enjoy
this quietness in God's love. While the Lord might well
give us a tasty morsel, a word of life full of insight, in the
course of five or ten minutes of *lectio*, to receive the
refreshment to which the Lord invites us – 'Come to me all
you who labour and are heavily burdened and I will
refresh you.'[2] – most people need at least twenty minutes.
The common tradition of all religions calls for such prayer
in the morning and in the evening. Thus the recommended
period is twenty minutes twice a day.

We settle ourselves so that the body can be well rested
while the spirit rests in God. For most of us this means
sitting, the back well supported, feet on the ground, eyes
gently closed.

Settled, we turn in faith to God dwelling within – 'The
Father and I will come and make our home in you.'[3] We
give ourselves over completely to God in love. To abide
there quietly with God in love we use one simple word of

love: God, Lord, Jesus, love. . . . Just one simple word. We simply want to rest in God's love. Whenever anything else catches our attention, we simply return to the Lord using our word of love. Some days we will not need to use our word much; on other days we will need to repeat it almost constantly. No matter. We are there with the Lord in love.

At the end of our appointed time, we do well to end our prayer gently. I suggest praying the Lord's prayer, very quietly and slowly, phrase by phrase, letting each open itself out as much as it wants.

This quiet resting in the Lord is doing the most we can to enter into true contemplation. For the rest, it is God's doing. The Lord can draw us deeply into himself. Or God can leave us there, longing for him, using our word repeatedly to return. All sorts of thoughts, feelings, memories may come up. As we return to the Lord with our word, they pass away and with them some of the inner tension attached to them. Memory wounds are healed. We are refreshed on many levels of our being. The Lord is true to his word.

A Rule of Life

To find a regular place in our life for *lectio* and contemplative prayer, to have a peaceful and orderly life within which the Lord can be present to us, it is almost essential that we have a personal rule of life. The rule needs to be such as supports our doing what we really want to do, our being who we really want to be. At the same time it has to be realistic. Therefore it has to be flexible and regularly refurbished.

To formulate a personal rule of life, I would suggest we

begin with some ardent prayer to Holy Spirit for guidance and insight. Then I would suggest taking four sheets of paper.

On the first sheet we seek to list all the things we really want. We all want to be happy. But to be happy we have to know what we want, and know that we have it or are on the way to getting it. What do you want? Write it all down.

On the second sheet we list all that we have to have and do to get what we want. I want to get enough sleep. For me that means getting six hours a night. What does it mean for you?

As we approach the third sheet we cast a glance over our shoulder. What in the past few months has been keeping me from being happy, from doing what I want to do, getting what I want to get? The moment might come for us to pray the serenity prayer: 'Lord, give me the courage to change the things I can change; the serenity to accept the things I can't change; and the wisdom to know the difference.'

Finally we come to the fourth sheet. And here is the true challenge. We formulate a programme for ourselves on a daily, weekly and monthly basis. A monthly day of retreat when we refurbish our rule of life is a good idea. We will obviously find that all that we want will not fit into a twenty-four-hour day or a seven-day week. Here we must make choices. Giving up the good to keep the better. If we can really give up the good, at least for now, these desires will no longer remain in our lives as unfulfilled wants that sap our joy and our energy. We will be freer to do the better, the things we really want and we will know a new joy and empowerment.

The creation of a rule of life will not be an easy matter, especially the first time. But if we persist we will come to know it as something that truly liberates, an instrument of joy. One of the reasons why Cistercians are such happy people is because they live under a Rule and an *abba*. If part of your rule is to meet with a spiritual father or mother or companion on the way on your monthly retreat day, this will multiply your joy.

Appendix 1

THE METHOD OF *LECTIO*

It is well to keep the Sacred Scriptures enthroned in our home in a place of honour as a Real Presence of the Word in our midst.

- Take the Sacred Text with reverence and call upon Holy Spirit.

- For ten minutes (or longer, if you are so drawn) listen to the Lord speaking to you through the Text, and respond to him.

- At the end of the time, choose a word or phrase (perhaps one will have been 'given' to you) to take with you and thank the Lord for being with you and speaking to you.

More briefly we might put it this way:

- Come into the Presence and call upon Holy Spirit.

- Listen for ten minutes.

- Thank the Lord and take a 'word'.

Appendix 2

CENTERING PRAYER

Sit relaxed and quiet.

- Be in faith and love to God who dwells in the centre of your being.

- Take up a love word and let it be gently present, supporting your being to God in faith-filled love.

- Whenever you become aware of anything, simply, gently return to the Lord with the use of your prayer word.

After twenty minutes let the Our Father (or some other prayer) pray itself.

Some Helpful Reading

Aelred of Rievaulx, *The Works of Aelred of Rievaulx*, tr. Theodore Berkeley and others, Spencer MA – Kalamazoo MI: Cistercian Publications, 1969–.

Benedict of Nursia, *Rule for Monasteries* in *RB 1980*, Timothy Fry (ed.), Collegeville MN: The Liturgical Press, 1981.

Bernard of Clairvaux, *The Works of Bernard of Clairvaux*, tr. Michael Casey and others, Spencer MA – Kalamazoo MI: Cistercian Publications, 1969–.

Casey, Michael, *Sacred Reading. The Ancient Art of Lectio Divina*, Melbourne: HarperCollins, 1995.

DeGanck, Roger, *Beatrice of Nazareth in her Context*, Cistercian Studies Series 121, Kalamazoo MI: Cistercian Publications, 1991.

—*Towards Unification with God*, Cistercian Studies Series 122, Kalamazoo MI: Cistercian Publications, 1991.

de Waal, Esther, *The Way of Simplicity: the Cistercian Tradition*, Darton Longman & Todd, 1998.

Elder, E. Rozanne (ed.), *The Contemplative Path*, Cistercian Studies Series 147, Kalamazoo MI: Cistercian Publications, 1995.

Finnegan, Sr Mary Jeremy, *Scholars and Mystics*, Chicago: Regnery, 1962.

Gertrude the Great of Helfta, *The Herald of God's Loving*

Kindness, Cistercian Fathers Series 35, tr. Alexandra Barratt, Kalamazoo MI: Cistercian Publications, 1991.

—*Spiritual Exercises*, Cistercian Fathers Series 49, tr. Gertrude Jaron Lewis and Jack Lewis, Kalamazoo MI: Cistercian Publications, 1989.

Guerric of Igny, *Liturgical Sermons*, Cistercian Fathers Series 8 and 32, tr. Monks of Mount St Bernard Abbey, Spencer MA: Cistercian Publications, 1970–1971.

Illich, Ivan, *In the Vineyard of the Text. A Commentary to Hugh's Didascalion*, Chicago: The University of Chicago Press, 1993.

Keating, Thomas, *Invitation to Love: The Way of Christian Contemplation*. New York: Continuum, 1992.

—*Open Mind, Open Heart: The Contemplative Dimension of the Gospels*, New York: Continuum, 1986.

Kline, Francis, *Lovers of the Place: Monasticism Loose in the Church*, Collegeville MN: Liturgical Press, 1997.

Leclercq, Jean, *Bernard of Clairvaux and the Cistercian Spirit*, Cistercian Studies Series 16, Kalamazoo MI: Cistercian Publications, 1975.

—*A Second Look at Saint Bernard*, Cistercian Studies Series 105. Kalamazoo MI: Cistercian Publications, 1990.

—*Women and Saint Bernard*, Cistercian Studies Series 104, Kalamazoo MI: Cistercian Publications, 1989.

McGuire, Brian Patrick, *The Difficult Saint: Saint Bernard and His Times*, Cistercian Studies Series 126, Kalamazoo MI: Cistercian Publications, 1991.

Merton, Thomas, *The Last of the Fathers*, New York: Harcourt Brace and World, 1954. This volume includes a translation of Pope Pius XII's Encyclical *Mellifluus Doctor*.

—*Opening the Bible*, Collegeville MI: The Liturgical Press, 1970.

—*Thomas Merton on Saint Bernard,* Cistercian Studies Series 9, Kalamazoo MI: Cistercian Publications, 1980.

Pennington, M. Basil, *A Place Apart*, Liguori MO: Liguori, 1998.

—*Bernard of Clairvaux. A Lover Teaching the Way of Love*, Hyde Park NY: New City Press, 1997.

—*Bernard of Clairvaux. A Saint's Life in Word and Image,* Huntington IN: Our Sunday Visitor, 1994.

—*The Cistercians*, Collegeville MN: Liturgical Press, 1992.

—*Last of the Fathers. The Cistercian Fathers of the Twelfth Century*, Still River MA: St Bede's, 1983.

—*Lectio Divina. Renewing the Ancient Practice of Praying the Scriptures,* New York: Crossroad, 1998.

—*Light from the Cloister. A Practical Spirituality for Practical Christians Inspired by Monastic Practice*, New York: Paulist, 1991.

—*Saint Bernard of Clairvaux, Studies Commemorating the Eighth Centenary of his Canonization,* Cistercian Studies Series 28, Kalamazoo MI: Cistercian Publications, 1977.

—*Thomas Merton Brother Monk. The Quest for True Freedom*, New York: Continuum, 1997.

—*Thomas Merton My Brother. His Journey to Freedom, Compassion and Final Integration*, Hyde Park NY: New City Press, 1996.

—*William of Saint Thierry. The Way to Divine Union*, Hyde Park, NY: New City Press, 1998.

Pranger, M. B., *Bernard of Clairvaux and the Shape of Monastic Thoughts: Broken Dreams,* Leiden: Brill, 1994.

Shank, Lillian Thomas and John Nichols, *Hidden Springs. Cistercian Monastic Women,* 2 vols, Cistercian Studies Series 113, Kalamazoo MI: Cistercian Publications, 1995.

Sommerfeldt, John R., *The Spiritual Teaching of Saint Bernard*, Cistercian Studies Series 125, Kalamazoo MI: Cistercian Publications, 1995.

William of Saint Thierry, *The Works of William of Saint Thierry*, tr. Penelope Lawson and others, Spencer MA – Kalamazoo MI: Cistercian Publications, 1969–.

Notes

Introduction

1. Lillian Thomas Shank and John Nichols, *Hidden Springs. Cistercian Monastic Women*, 2 vols, Cistercian Studies Series 113, Kalamazoo MI: Cistercian Publications, 1995.

1 A Spirit is Enkindled

1. Benedict of Nursia, *Rule for Monasteries* (hereafter *RB*), 58:7.
2. Psalm 50/51:17.
3. *The Little Exordium* 15 in M. Basil Pennington, *The Cistercians*, Collegeville MN: Liturgical Press, p. 107.
4. Ibid., pp. 97–109.

2 For Beginners: William of Saint Thierry

1. William of Saint Thierry, *On Contemplating God* (hereafter *CG*) 1.
2. Ibid.
3. *CG* 10.
4. Ibid.
5. John 17:21.
6. *CG* 11.
7. *CG* 12.
8. Ibid.
9. William of Saint Thierry, *The Nature and Dignity of Love* (hereafter *NDL*), 1.

10. Ibid.
11. Ibid.
12. *NDL* 2.
13. *NDL* 3.
14. Ibid.
15. *NDL* 4.
16. *NDL* 10.
17. *NDL* 12.
18. *NDL* 14.
19. Ibid.
20. Ibid.
21. Ibid.
22. *NDL* 21.
23. Ibid.
24. Ibid.
25. *NDL* 23.
26. *NDL* 25.
27. *NDL* 26.
28. *NDL* 35.
29. *NDL* 38.
30. Ibid., 44.
31. Ibid.
32. *NDL* 45.
33. Ibid.
34. Ibid.
35. Psalm 27/26:8.
36. RB 58:7.
37. Romans 9:15f. in William of Saint Thierry, *Meditations*
    (hereafter *Med.*), 1:1.
38. Romans 9:19f. in *Med.* 1:2.
39. *Med.* 1:3.
40. *Med.* 1:9; cf. Augustine, *In Joan.*, 26, 2.
41. *Med.* 11:1.
42. *Med.* 11:1f.
43. Hebrews 4:12.
44. *Med.* 11:13.

45. *Med.* 11:15.
46. *Med.* 11:16.
47. *Med.* 11:17.
48. *Med.* 12:2.
49. *Med.* 12:5.
50. *Med.* 12:8.
51. *Med.* 12:10.
52. *Med.* 12:18.
53. William of Saint Thierry, *Exposition on the Song of Songs* (hereafter *Song*), Pref. 5.
54. *Song* 143.
55. *Song* 95 and 99.
56. *Song* 92.
57. Ibid.
58. *Song* 94.
59. *Song* 97.
60. *Song* 123.
61. Ibid.
62. *Song* 127.
63. *Song* 107.
64. *Song* 117ff.
65. *Song* 141f.
66. *Song* 146.
67. *Song* 203.
68. William of Saint Thierry, *Mirror of Faith* (hereafter *Mir.*) 6.
69. *Mir.* 3.
70. *Mir.* 13.
71. *Mir.* 5.
72. *Mir.* 8.
73. *Mir.* 11.
74. *Mir.* 11 and 15.
75. *Mir.* 25f.
76. *Mir.* 11.
77. *Mir.* 30.
78. *Mir.* 32.

79. *Mir.* 19ff.
80. Ibid.
81. *Mir.* 19.
82. *Mir.* 32.
83. Ibid.
84. William of Saint Thierry, *The Enigma of Faith* (hereafter *Enigma*), 74.
85. *Enigma* 40–73.
86. *Enigma* 90.
87. William of Saint Thierry, *The Golden Epistle* (hereafter *GE*), Pref. 2.
88. *GE* 41.
89. *GE* 44.
90. *GE* 43ff.
91. Romans 12:3.
92. 1 Corinthians 24.
93. Galatians 3:5; *GE* 70f.
94. *GE* 81.
95. *GE* 109.
96. *GE* 89.
97. *GE* 93.
98. *GE* 132ff.
99. *GE* 179.
100. *GE* 177.
101. *GE* 182.
102. *GE* 227.
103. *GE* 249.
104. *GE* 257.
105. *GE* 263.
106. *GE* 265f.
107. *GE* 267.
108. *GE* 272f.
109. *GE* 286f.
110. *GE* 293.
111. *GE* 299.

3 *The Way of Friendship: Aelred of Rievaulx*

1. Aelred of Rievaulx, *Mirror of Charity* (hereafter *MC*), 1:1.
2. *MC* 1:8.
3. *MC* 1:11f.
4. *MC* 1:14.
5. *MC* 1:24.
6. *MC* 1:27.
7. *MC* 2:3f.
8. *MC* 1:88f., 92.
9. 1 John 2:16.
10. *MC* 2:25.
11. *MC* 2:26.
12. Ibid.
13. *MC* 2:49.
14. *MC* 2:50.
15. *MC* 3:1: Leviticus 23:3; 25:3f., 8, 10.
16. *MC* 3:3.
17. *MC* 3:5.
18. *MC* 3:49.
19. *MC* 3:108.
20. *MC* 3:110.
21. *MC* 3:109.
22. Aelred of Rievaulx, *Spiritual Friendship* (hereafter *SF*), 1:10ff.
23. *SF* 1:32.
24. *SF* 1:38f.
25. *SF* 1:42.
26. *SF* 1:45.
27. *SF* 2:19ff.
28. *SF* 1:69f.
29. *SF* 3:79f.
30. *SF* 3:132f.
31. *SF* 3:5.
32. *SF* 3:51.

33. *SF* 3:55f.
34. *SF* 3:82.
35. Psalm 72:22.
36. *SF* 3:119ff.

4 *Everyday Holiness: Guerric of Igny*

1. Ezekiel 40:37.
2. Sirach 44:6.
3. Sermon 53:2f.
4. Sermon 53:5.
5. Sermon 22:5.
6. Sermon 54:5.
7. Ibid.
8 Psalm 119:129.
9 Sirach 24:27. It is interesting to note here that Guerric attributes to Jesus the words of the Wise Man. Sermon 54:2.
10. 1 Thessalonians 4:11.
11. Sermon 49:5.
12. Sermon 49:6.
13. Ibid.

5 *The Master of the School: Bernard of Clairvaux*

1. Luke 1:27; Bernard of Clairvaux, *In Praise of the Virgin Mary* 2:17.
2. Luke 1:28.
3. Luke 1:30; Bernard of Clairvaux, *Sermon for the Nativity of the Blessed Virgin Mary* 6.
4. Proverbs 6:12f.
5. Bernard of Clairvaux, *Sermons on the Song of Songs* (hereafter *SSS*), 1:7.
6. Proverbs 4:23.
7. Genesis 3:19.
8. Bernard of Clairvaux, *The Steps of Humility and Pride*, 28.

9. Psalm 115:10.
10. Matthew 5:7.
11. *The Steps of Humility and Pride*, 15ff.
12. Bernard of Clairvaux, *Grace and Free Choice*, 7.
13. *Grace and Free Choice*, 9.
14. *SSS* 3:5.

6 *Let's Be Practical – Very Practical*

1. Psalm 46:10
2. Matthew 11:28.
3. John 14:23.